Woman
by Divine Design

Dr. Jeffrey L. Seif
and Sandra Levitt

Woman By Divine Design

All rights reserved.
Copyright 2007 by Zola Levitt Ministries, Inc.
10300 North Central Expressway, Suite 170
Dallas, Texas 75231
214-696-8844
www.levitt.com

ISBN 978-1-930749-45-0

This book may not be reproduced in whole or in part without permission of the publisher, except in cases of brief quotation embodied in critical articles or reviews.

Sandra's Dedication

I would like to dedicate this book:

To all the women in my life who have made me who I am today. Thank you for being God's women.

To my late husband, Zola, for teaching me how to be the woman I am today.

And to my son Will, who is the future.

Table of Contents

Introduction by Jeff, 1
The Misunderstanding, 1
The History: The Idea's Origin, 7
The Purpose: *Why* a Book on Women?, 8
The Process: *How* We Intend to Explore Women's Issues, 10

Jesus and Women, 13
Introduction, 13
Jesus and Women in Mark's Gospel, 17
Jesus and Women in Matthew's Gospel, 23
Jesus and Women in Luke's Gospel, 37
Jesus and Women in John's Gospel, 47
Summary: Jesus and Women in the Gospels, 53

Paul and Women, 55
Introduction, 55
Galatians, 59
1 and 2 Thessalonians, 61
1 and 2 Corinthians, 63
Romans, 69
Philemon, 73
Colossians, 75
Ephesians, 77
Philippians, 81
1 Timothy, 83
Titus, 91
2 Timothy, 93
Summary: Paul and Women, 95

Conclusion, 97

Table of Contents

Endnotes, 103

Glossary of Women, 105

Study Guide, 115

Introduction by Jeff

The Misunderstanding
According to the Hebrew Bible, "in the beginning" God created man. But man was lonely with only fur and feathers as companions. So, from man, God fashioned a woman who, in turn, became man's mate (Gen. 1:26-27; 2:18-25; cf. 7:1-2 [Editor's Note: cf.=*compare with*]). With Eve's glorious form in full view, Gen. 2:23 says the world's first man exclaimed: "This is now bone of my bones and flesh of my flesh; she shall be called woman." He who was made in God's image now saw a related image that fired his imagination. After experiencing love at first sight, the first man and woman entered into a mysterious fellowship called matrimony and settled in to find a life together in the brave new world.

Men's enthusiasm at the sight of women's forms and features resonates throughout the biblical narrative—in Genesis and beyond.

Like Adam before him, Abraham noted in Gen. 12:11 that Sarah was "beautiful to look at." In like manner, in 24:16 Old Testament readers are introduced to Isaac's bride-to-be, Rebekah, who, according to the Sacred Text, was "very beautiful, a virgin." Like his progenitors, the patriarch Jacob experienced a wellspring of emotion and a surge of energy when he first saw Rachel. In Gen. 29:17 we are told that she was "lovely in form and beautiful." As with his fathers, he was anxious to get to *know* this person who was the object of his attention, in the biblical way that is.

The Sacred Scripture's opening narratives observe that *males chose females, in part, on the basis of physical desirability.* Not recognizing this sexual attraction as sacred, the notion doesn't sit well with some—but this sort of discrimination is just the beginning of our misunderstanding.

According to Dr. Milton Fisher of the Reformed Episcopal Seminary, the Old Testament's word translated "female" is derived from a Hebrew root meaning to "pierce" or to "bore"[1]—a connotation which, at the first, seems a bit disturbing. Is the Bible laying credence to women's being sexual objects—to "bore"? The words employed here seem pretty graphic.

The New Testament's word for "female," as in Mk. 10:6; Matt. 19:4; Gal. 3:28; Rom. 1:26-27, is a bit better—but *not* much. It comes from a root meaning "nipple," to "give suck,"[2] and speaks of nurturing or what we call "mothering." With the Old Testament's root, it carries implications for classifications that, at first, *seem* limiting and disparaging.

Introduction by Jeff

What might one make of this?

Were women manufactured from men to be gratification objects for men? Do the Scriptures suggest that women are merely utilities through whom the favored men produce and rear their young? If so, would it not be better to be born male? If so, one wonders how women could view the Scriptures as a helpful guidebook if it discriminates for or against them on the basis of perceived beauty and then marginalizes the pretty "chosen" one as simply a form of male property.

Is this the biblical record's testimony? No!

Though not an expert on the morphology of words or linguistics, I am of the understanding that primitive words developed to give voice to basic needs and interests. Sexual inclinations and sociological norms understandably factored into primitive expressions that defined relationships, which, in turn, spelled out basic human functions and interactions. I thus conclude that though the words' ancient etymologies may sound offensive to modern sensibilities, we do well to reserve rushing to judgment and understand that the ancient language draws upon function.

Furthermore, the Text does not single out and objectify women. Consider the biblical word for "beautiful"—*yapha*. It is also employed for "handsome" and is used to describe men as well: Joseph was noted as being "well-built and handsome" (Gen. 39:6). When Bible readers first cast their eyes upon David, they meet someone described in the Text as "ruddy, with beautiful eyes, and handsome" (1 Sam. 16:12).

For that matter, the seemingly discriminatory language of form and function is not even limited to females and males; God, Himself, is described in Sacred Scripture on the utilitarian basis of what He does—e.g., He is a "God of War," "God the Provider," etc. Speaking of utility, women admit to choosing men, in part, based on how well they can provide: he wants beauty; she wants security. The point here is that the Bible does not single out women for judgments.

To my way of thinking, much of the offense results because biblical literature's valuation of women, as practiced by Jesus and Moses, has been contradicted by the historical interpretation of the Apostle Paul's letters to his churches, leading those who value women to opine that women would fare better were they unshackled from the fetters of Paul, said to impose a narrow vision for women's reality and to consequently restrict women's chances for personal happiness. Most readers of the English language Bible can discern two distinct messages: one in the Gospel of Jesus, the other in the letters of Paul.

Those who shun the Bible's teachings as suspicious because of its instruction to women are in danger of throwing out the baby (the Gospel of Jesus) with the bathwater (Paul's letters) because someone *told* them that the bathwater was muddy. This is a great disservice to women as it distances

Introduction by Jeff

them from the protection of a system that we will see is designed to protect both their welfare and men's. How do women fare when separated from the basic values taught in the Bible? Let's look at the world beyond biblical influence and see.

In November 2005, BBC News reported the results of the World Health Organization's survey of 24,000 women in ten not-particularly-Christian countries, and informed that, on the average, one in six women (17%) suffered "intimate partner abuse." The BBC claimed that women in poorer countries fare worse than women in wealthier ones, citing another WHO study that found that 15% of Japanese women suffered from domestic violence compared to 71% of Ethiopian women. Of women surveyed in Bangladesh, Ethiopia, Peru, and Tanzania, 30%-54% reported being abused during the previous year alone. A survey of 8,000 Turkish housewives revealed that about half of them believed they actually "deserved to be beaten" if they "argued with their husbands" or "refused to give them sex." Drawing on an Amnesty International report, the BBC had reported five months earlier (in May 2005) that a third of Nigerian women experienced spousal abuse and accepted it as normal. Add to all of this the fact that two million young girls experience genital mutilation annually in Africa and the non-Jewish Middle East, and that 5,000 brides are burned each year in India, freeing husbands to find other brides and dowries. The crimes of "honor killings" and forced marriage have spread even into the heart of the West, including London and Paris, as immigrants from

Woman By Divine Design

outside the Judeo-Christian influence cling to traditions that treat women as mere property. Hundreds of thousands of women are sold every year as sex slaves in Thailand and elsewhere. One is forced to conclude that, beyond the sphere of biblical influence, *a devastation of global proportions is being wreaked upon womankind*, exacting a toll that surpasses the annual carnage caused by hurricanes, earthquakes, tsunamis, and even incessant political violence!

So, do women fare better, or even as well, in a world outside biblical influence? Seems not. I would like to cast a vision of what the Bible *really* intends for womankind. And I believe that I had better do it quickly, because another worldview is competing for our attention.

Tragically, many Europeans long ago abandoned their Christian faith and values for secularism. Now, with nothing to live, die, or fight for, their lethargic complacency is all too easily exploited by Islamic strategists bent on spreading their culture and values into the West. Already, we are hearing the hoofbeats of apocalyptic horses pounding the pavement in Europe, where European earth is being shaken by Islamic-inspired anti-Semitism. Coupled with this, we are hearing more and more reports that women are miserably mistreated in Islamic culture: that women are sorely oppressed and subjugated therein; that women generally lack upward mobility; that women are often deprived of education; that women are construed as the property of husbands, who can easily discipline and dispose of them and

Introduction by Jeff

replace them with younger wives; that women are beaten; and that many women live without hope in this world, as a result of this culture.

Even if one assumes that the aforementioned WHO and BBC numbers are inflated for political purposes, *one cannot deny that women's experience in modernity is wrought with many perils.* This being the case, we intend to show how the Bible's call for men to protect women, to honor marriage, and to esteem motherhood works toward women's welfare and happiness. This book examines God's ideal design for social and church order and explores aspects of the truly liberating biblical testimony.

The History:
The Idea's Origin

Much as many women have difficultly, globally, I have discovered that developing a study of women's experience is itself wrought with as many criticisms as it promises possibilities.

Newly installed as our ministry's spiritual leader and its principal theologian and spokesman, I was anxious to teach Scripture and to cast vision for the ministry's future. In response to my television co-host's interest in developing a women's series, I mentioned in our newsletter that we were contemplating such. Boy, did I get some negative mail! "A woman is taking over the ministry," some accused —a reference to Sandra Levitt's alleged control; others said we were "hijacked by the feminist agenda;" others claimed we had "lost our way," and the like. Frankly, I really did not expect this at all. I thought those people were being mean and petty, and I was itching to respond. But, I wanted to do so kindly and effectively.

The Purpose:
Why a Book on Women?

As a street cop, I responded to domestic abuse just about every time I put on a police uniform. I often privately lamented that some women seemed to get a raw deal, and as a police officer, I could at least take the violator to jail and "throw the book at him." I knew he'd just get out and beat her up again. But what could I do? Memories of those domestic incidents remain indelibly marked in my mind's eye, the vivid images haunting me to this day. My research at the helm of Zola Levitt Ministries has brought me face to face with devastating pictures of women's experience in Islamic-controlled cultures. Here, as before, I find myself confronted by abusive images that I find quite disturbing. It brings out the cop in me!

Remembering previous police experiences and taking notice of what I construe as the unfortunate plight of many hundreds of millions of Muslim women on our planet, *it started to occur to me that casting a biblical vision of women's reality might be not just a good idea, but an extremely important one*—for Muslim women who haven't met Jesus, for Christian women who have turned their backs on Paul, and for their sisters who reject Christianity outright because of the confusing messages delivered through Paul's main interpreter, the

Introduction by Jeff

Church. I realized that Sandra was onto something big and, with her, I started to think that this was a great time to tell the story.

The team started putting creative energies to work on what we began to recognize as an extremely important television series. In the course of preparing, I went through the Bible and located eight women-related areas that I thought were worthy of exploring in a television series. Our producer, Ken Berg, agreed, as did Sandra, who weighed in on my framework. Mark Levitt, the ministry's financial steward, increased the production budget for the series, creating more energy in the dramatic production and allowing for more actors and a longer shooting schedule. *We wanted to do it right, believing that the world's women and Christianity's message to them are worth it.* Sandra caught on film great interviews with women who are really making a difference in Israel—even interviewing my wife, Patty, on camera. The upshot of it all is that, with God's help, we put together what I consider our best television series to date—an absolutely fantastic series entitled: *She Shall Be Called Woman.* The video series focuses primarily on women of the Old Testament. To complement the series with a New Testament perspective, we got to work on a book—this book: *Woman By Divine Design.* In what follows, I'll delineate the book's particulars and let you know how Sandra and I worked on it.

Woman By Divine Design

The Process:
How We Intend to Explore Women's Issues

This volume is principally concerned with one question: *What kind of vision does the Bible cast for women's experience?*

In the interest of tendering a cogent response, I was anxious to come to terms with (1) where, (2) when, and (3) how Jesus interacted with women in the Gospel traditions—thinking we would do well to take our lead from Him. Additionally, I thought it would be helpful to come to terms with (4) how the Gospel's principal interpreter, Paul, understood and interacted with women. Often misinterpreted as being against womankind, his writings required a closer examination and I was anxious to see if a Jewish studies approach might assist us to draw a more accurate picture of Paul and his relationship with women. (5) Considering the context within which Paul ministered would help us understand his Texts. Therefore, I applied myself to offer some samplings of that as well.

Sandra's idea and my theological research resulted in a first draft of the manuscript—which I handed over to Sandra for her energies and insights. She addressed the issues from a woman's perspective and, as an educator, took particular interest in ensuring that there would be sufficient means to facilitate readers' learning. In this and other ways, Sandra's expertise is evident and her reflections were absorbed into the volume's essence and substance. With both of us having weighed in on the issues from our distinct perspectives, the manuscript was sent to our editor,

Introduction by Jeff

Margot Dokken; next to the printer, and now it is in your hands.

Blessings to you as you consider *Woman By Divine Design*. We hope you'll be as blessed by it as we are by presenting it to you.

Jeffrey L. Seif   Tel Aviv, Israel
                                                     June 2007

Jesus and Women

Introduction

As with women's studies generally, the prospect of coming to terms with Jesus' relationship with women presents a host of problems and possibilities.

In this case, problems abound because we really don't know—the records don't tell us—everything that Jesus did with, or said to or about women. The lack of source material contributes to uncertainty. Happily, there are possibilities because we do have some insightful biblical samplings to work with.

As we shall see, the New Testament samplings that are available afford interpreters the opportunity to focus attention on Jesus and women, and then offer tentative reconstructions on the basis of what He is purported to have said, what His sayings might have meant, how He said what He said, and how He interacted with women, generally. Due to our interest in issues associated with women and "Divine design," an introductory study of Jesus' relationship with women is deemed important—for, according to biblical literature, He is woman's Divine

Woman By Divine Design

co-Designer and Creator (Jn. 1:1-5; cf. Gen. 1:26-27). For these and other reasons, Jesus' relationship with women will be the object of our attention here.

This chapter will be guided by the following questions: Where in the New Testament was Jesus noted talking to, for, and/or about women? What did He say? How did He say it? What did His sayings really mean yesterday? What might they mean today? How do the Gospel writers position Jesus with respect to women? Does Jesus come off as being aloof or congenial? Friendly or unfriendly? Is He comfortable or seemingly uncomfortable? Close or distant? What of women and their relationship to Him? In the Gospel traditions, do women seem comfortable with Jesus? Are women approached by Him and do they construe Him as approachable?

At the outset—and at the risk of throwing a potentially disorienting academic wrench into the machinery—let us inform that we, the authors, subscribe to what scholars call the "Marcan Priority Hypothesis." Argued by means of this "hypothesis" (theory) is that *Mark* (a non-Apostle who happened to be Peter's associate) *wrote his Gospel narrative first,* and that the *others eventually followed with theirs, utilizing his Text* in the process. Those who find this odd do well to look at Luke. In 1:1-3, Luke explicitly noted that he had the other documents on hand when writing. Of importance to us is how Matthew and Luke added known women's stories as they worked and re-presented Mark's initial draft.

Jesus and Women

Matthew's Gospel contains 1,068 verses, 500 of which are found in Mark and 235 more of which are found in Luke. If one does the math, *only 333—less than a third—of Matthew's 1,068 verses are unique to Matthew.* Luke's is the longest Gospel, with 1,149 verses, 350 of which are found in Mark, 235 in Matthew. The upshot here is that *of Luke's 1,149 verses, only 564—less than half—are unique to Luke's Gospel.* Because of their similar content, Matthew, Mark, and Luke are called the "synoptic" Gospels.

John's Gospel stands in marked contrast to the synoptic Gospels, with little sharing of source material, though there is some sharing. A treatment of the documents' interrelationships is marginal for our purposes, save noting the fact that, *with the passage of time, there seemed to be a growing interest in filling the narratives with Jesus-and-women stories.* This will be evident as we consider the Gospels individually.

Now let's look at Jesus and women in the various Gospel narratives.

Jesus and Women – Mark's Gospel

Jesus and Women in Mark's Gospel

In 1:29-31, Mark noted that Peter's mother-in-law was stricken with a "fever," and that Jesus helped her get the better of her affliction. Jesus is said to have healed her and, in the wake of His so doing, "she served them" in return (v. 31). Not much is said of her beyond this.

In chapter 5, Mark gave a more detailed accounting of Jesus' brief encounters with two women—one young and the other older—and these combined stories give interpreters more material for investigation.

These stories begin with a vexed synagogue "ruler" named Jairus, who was broken by the ill health of his little girl. She was dying (v. 23) and her concerned father was unable to marshal conventional resources to help her get the better of her problem. With word of Jesus' abilities spreading far and wide, Jairus opted to petition Him for His unconventional assistance. In v. 22, he came and fell at Jesus' feet, and in v. 23 "begged Him earnestly" to come and heal his daughter. Jesus did (v. 41).

While Jesus was en route to attend to Jairus' business, Mark noted that a sickly woman with a blood-related problem followed in the crowd—a grown woman, in this case. Unlike the little girl, she had no well-placed "ruler," no male protector to advocate for her. She was all alone—and in dire trouble.

Ostracized as a result of an incessant flow of blood, this wretched woman was deemed an unwanted "untouchable."

Woman By Divine Design

Rendered "unclean," the outcast was forbidden any and all contact with males. Even a kindly, sympathetic hug was forbidden as she was deemed a contaminant. Lonely and desperate and having had enough after twelve years of this, she opted to throw the day's decorum to the wind. Convinced that by touching even the fringe of this wonder-working-rabbi's garment she could secure the desired outcome—a healing—she decided to touch Jesus (vv. 27-28).

Hoping to go unnoticed, she opted to make her move while Jesus was being jostled about, making His way through a swelling crowd. She snuck in there and did it—and thought she got away with it. Amidst the hustle and bustle of the press of many people, Jesus turned about, looked her way and thundered, "Who touched me?" (vv. 30-31). The disciples made light of the question, given that so many were pushing against Him (v. 31); but Jesus pressed the matter. In response to His persistence, finally the "woman, knowing what had happened to her," and what she had done to make it happen, "came and fell at His feet and, trembling with fear, told Him the whole truth" (v. 33). The woman with the flow of blood was "caught red-handed." She knew she'd been healed; but this seemed to be the beginning of a new set of troubles.

She had seen an opportunity to go unnoticed, but it was risky—and inappropriate.

Jesus "called her out" and she knew she was "in for it." *This desperate, dirty, unclean thing had touched a miracle-*

Jesus and Women – Mark's Gospel

working rabbi, and she was going to hear about it. She preferred to remain hidden, but Jesus would not allow it.

Her world was about to fall apart—or so she thought. Jesus didn't rebuke her; to the contrary, He countered with, "Daughter, your faith has made you well. Go in peace and be healed of your affliction" (v. 34). This response is striking for a few reasons.

Jesus' brief address to her betrays a kindly and tender disposition, does it not? It shows His concern for a woman who had not been touched by any man in any way for twelve years. In that He had already healed her, and she knew it, His "Go be healed of your affliction" seems superfluous. It isn't.

In Luke 8:44, readers are told that she was healed "immediately." Why then did Jesus send her off with "Go be healed of your affliction"? It may have been His assuring her that the problem wouldn't come back: His healing was permanent. That aside, His calling this pushy, grown woman a "daughter" is striking, in part, because He was on His way to a powerful man's daughter to assist her, something He chose to do at the synagogue ruler's beckoning. Against that backdrop, this abandoned woman became Jesus' daughter. That Jesus attended to both the dispossessed and the powerful, the well placed and the displaced, is good news for all women (and men).

Speaking of "all," a comparable story follows.

Woman By Divine Design

In 7:24-30, Mark recorded a fascinating interaction between Jesus and a non-Jewish woman. As with the previous accounts, here too *Jesus is shown as being kindly disposed toward an untouchable*—a non-Jewish, Syro-Phoenician "dog."

Mark said that "He entered a house and wanted no one to know it" (7:24). This must have been the sort of house that Jewish men like Jesus weren't supposed to enter. Objections to His so doing notwithstanding, He came at the beckoning of a Greek woman who "fell at His feet" and petitioned Him for assistance with her demon-possessed daughter. One should not "take the children's bread and throw it to their dogs," in v. 27, was Jesus' seemingly offhanded reply. Jesus, however, healed the little girl in vv. 29-30; and, by so doing, Jesus is on record noting that *He cared for all women, irrespective of race, class, or circumstance.* Jesus is shown as a protector of women, is He not?

Moving along, in chapter 10, Mark traced Jesus' footsteps as He made His way to Jerusalem for His personal rejection and for His appointment with His destiny. On the way, He discussed divorcement in vv. 1-12—divorce being an act that has devastating consequences, especially for women.

"Is it lawful for a man to divorce his wife?" asked some religious leaders (v. 2). In response to their testy question, Jesus appealed to Moses in v. 3, asking, "What did Moses command you?" They retorted that "Moses permitted a man to write a certificate of divorce and send her away"

Jesus and Women – Mark's Gospel

(v. 4). Jesus weighed in, saying that this was because of human "hardness" (v. 5), but that it was *never* God's plan from the beginning (vv. 6-9). Ditching women is not what God is about! Later, His disciples raised the issue again (v. 10); in response, Jesus pressed the point even further, expressing His will that *marriage be permanent*—period (vv.11-12). At issue here wasn't whether undesirable circumstances might afford both members of a couple the opportunity and the right to "file for divorce." Though the question of whether there are ever biblical grounds for legitimate divorce is worth considering—and we, the authors, do believe that there are such cases—we do well to note that this particular question was asked and answered in the context of whether a party can casually discard the other without just cause. The answer is an emphatic "no." It is but another example of Jesus championing women's interests and advocating for their security.

The women were loyal to Him to the end—and in a way that outshines the male disciples' performances: The book closed noting that Mary Magdalene, Mary the mother of James, and Salomé extended kindness toward Jesus' corpse and memory, with Mary Magdalene noted as the first to see the risen Lord (16:1-11).

These Spartan samplings are pretty much it for Mark's Gospel. Jesus doesn't speak much to or about women in Mark, or tackle women's issues; but what He does say and show are deemed to be quite significant in depicting Jesus as equally receptive and responsive to all women.

Jesus and Women – Matthew's Gospel

Jesus and Women in Matthew's Gospel

Unlike Mark—who offers only a few stories of Jesus' interactions with women, and is only concerned with stories of the adult Jesus—Matthew gives readers a narrative of Jesus' infancy, where he places a variety of women in the unfolding drama. Four women are noted in His birthing line in the first chapter: Tamar (1:3), Rahab (v. 5), Ruth (v. 5) and Bathsheba (v. 6). After these women are introduced in Jesus' genealogical record, His mother Mary appears in vv. 16-25.

Matthew introduces women right from the start. Who were these women?

According to Genesis 38:1ff. [Editor's Note: ff.=*and what follows*], Tamar was the terribly abused and disrespected daughter-in-law of Judah. Feeling uncomfortable, given that two of his sons had already died after marrying her, Judah wasn't about to let her marry the next, though he had promised and it was the custom of the day. Moses recorded that her husbands were worthless and wicked and really got what they deserved (vv. 7-10). However, their father, Judah, was in denial over this and, though innocent of any and all wrongdoing, Tamar was marginalized in the clan and tacitly blamed for the deaths of the pathetic men. Having no means to provide for her self or her future, she disguised herself and posed as a prostitute to secure an heir from within the family. With little effort, she secured Judah's affection for a moment and conceived a child through the less-than-desirable union—supporting the allegation that men all-too-readily give in to the temptations of sex and food. When word got out later that Judah's daughter-in-law had broken the law and was pregnant, Judah was indignant and ordered her put to death (v. 24). His anger was assuaged, however, when his being the father came to light, and he was humbled in the presence of everyone (v. 26). What became of the offspring of this disrespected woman? A son grew up to stand in the line as one of the progenitors of Israel's greatest Hebrew: the Messiah—Jesus.

Matthew continued his notation of the women in Jesus' family tree by picking up the story of another of his great-great-grandmothers: Rahab—a prostitute (v. 5a and Josh. 2:1b). What was her story? Rahab's entrance into the biblical narrative is played out against the backdrop of the following.

In the wake of Moses' passing, and immediately after assuming command of the Israelites and in advance of the initial conquest of Canaan, Joshua sent men to spy out the land (Josh. 2:1a). Wanting to hide their presence and not draw too much attention, the spies opted to dwell at the lodging of a known prostitute, Rahab, given that people would be used to seeing men come and go (v. 1b).

How did they find her house? Did they inquire in the town where traveling men might get "some action"? Perhaps. Who knows? How did this woman ever become a prostitute? The reasons why Rahab became a prostitute are not noted; what is noted, however, is that she was,

Jesus and Women – Matthew's Gospel

and that she was kindly disposed toward the Hebrews, that she helped them (vv. 3ff.), that she was spared in the carnage when the Israelites conquered (6:21-25), and that she eventually married into one of the clans after the fall of Jericho, giving birth to Boaz, who will be mentioned in a moment as one of those standing in the line of one of Israel's greatest Hebrews: the Messiah. God loved her and blessed her, did He not? God uses all for His glory, does He not?

Tamar posed as a prostitute; Rahab actually was one. Goodness! Are these not interesting women? The reasons why they are noted in Jesus' family line will be considered; first, let's look at another odd example. *The next mother in Jesus' family line was another non-virginal woman, a gentile named Ruth* (1:5).

The Old Testament informs that a man named Elimelech left Bethlehem for Moab with his wife, Naomi, and sons in tow (Ruth 1:1-2). The boys came of age and secured wives—of necessity, non-Jewish wives. Disconnected in Moab, the family was making a bid to garner some security in their new environment and marrying into non-Jewish families may well have been a practical step. Tragically for the family, however, Elimelech died, as did both boys shortly thereafter (vv. 3-5). Left destitute, and believing that the misfortune may well have been Divine retribution (1) for leaving the ancestral homeland in the first place, and (2) for violating God's commandments by giving her boys to non-Jewish girls, Naomi was minded to release her young daughters-in-law, Ruth and Orpah, from any

Woman By Divine Design

further obligations to her, and make her way back to Israel to finish her days among her own people. Orpah went home, but Ruth was determined to look after for Naomi.

The young and attractive Moabite girl was resolute and couldn't be shaken. Loyal, bold, and courageous, Ruth insisted that she would stay with her mother-in-law and her people, and that she would join herself to their God (vv. 16-18). That was that—period! Perceiving that Ruth's mind was set, Naomi did as she had intended, and virtuous Ruth went with her—with nothing but the promise of a peasant's existence to hope for.

They made their way back and, as expected, Ruth worked in the harvest as peasant help (2:1ff.). Industrious and beautiful—and this is always a catchy combination!—Ruth caught the attention of the wealthy landowner, Rahab's son Boaz. Anxious to look out for the interests of her adopted daughter, Naomi facilitated a union between the two, which was then made official (3:1-4:12). What became of the union between this gentile and this Jew? They bore a son—Obed, the father of Jesse, the father of David—who stood in the line of Israel's greatest Hebrew: the Messiah.

So what have we here—and in Jesus' direct family line, no less? We have a non-Jew, a prostitute, and a woman who posed as a prostitute! *There is no pretense at perfection, is there?* As interesting as all of this is, it pales in comparison to what follows. The next woman's story is so scandalous, Matthew couldn't even bring himself to mention her by

Jesus and Women – Matthew's Gospel

name—"Bathsheba." Knowing that everyone would know exactly whom he meant, he preferred to simply refer to her as she "who had been the wife of Uriah" (Matt. 1:6).

Samuel said that David went to his rooftop and let voyeuristic impulses get the better of him (2 Sam. 11: 2). His eyes alighted upon Bathsheba, the wife of Uriah the Hittite (v. 3). After inquiring about her—and perhaps thinking he could disrespect her because she was the wife of a gentile Hittite (despite his being a noble one)—on his own initiative, David opted to take her for himself while her noble husband was away fighting for him (v. 4; cf., vv. 1, 11). Tragic! What the king wanted, the king got. There was no resisting. It was as simple as that.

What complicated the matter, however, was that the woman became pregnant. Being unable to hide the affair from her husband—though he tried—David had him murdered, and then married his widow, Bathsheba (vv. 14-27) whom he had acquired under less-than-noble circumstances. The unnamed son died seven days after his birth. Readers are informed that later, the prophet Nathan confronted David (12:1-15). David could have killed him too; but happily for Nathan—and more so for David—the king repented of his sins and was forgiven (cf. Ps. 51:1ff.). Though God forgave him, his sons did not and family troubles followed him until his dying day (vv. 10-15). What became of the union of David and Bathsheba? Solomon was eventually born to them. Though Solomon's sexual appetite and indiscretions outshone his father's, the Grace of the Heavenly Father outperformed both, and Solomon grew up to stand in the line of Israel's greatest Hebrew: the Messiah (Matt. 1:6).

For her part, Bathsheba was a woman caught up in the middle of forces that she could not control. God providentially worked things for His own good and worked out His purposes through her, strange as His doing does indeed seem. Here in Jesus' lineage is but another example of God's Grace toward humankind, and His provision for women.

Is it not interesting that women would be noted in a patriarchal list? Much as all sorts of people constituted Jesus' lineage, so too, many kinds of people constitute His "offspring"—not just Jewish people. And so, after outlining three sections of fourteen varied names, Matthew finished his all-star line-up of women by focusing on Mary.

Matthew tells the story of the virgin Mary's betrothal to Joseph and the fact that her fiancé was crushed by discouragement upon learning that Mary had turned up pregnant—and not by him. Noting that he was basically "a just and good man," a gentle sort given to being kindly disposed toward the woman he surmised was given to wandering affections, Joseph was going to just walk away from her without making a scene (vv. 18-25, esp. v. 19).

It didn't quite happen that way, did it? An angel visited him in a dream and told him to "hold his peace" and keep with his initial plans, saying, "for the child within her has been conceived by the Holy Spirit" (v. 20). Not

Jesus and Women – Matthew's Gospel

wanting to argue with an angel—and believing in his heart, no doubt, that Mary truly was an "angel" herself—Joseph "awoke from his sleep and did as the angel of the Lord commanded him, and took Mary as his wife" (v. 24), and the union was not consummated until after the miracle-born child arrived (v. 25).

"Wise men" from the "east" were informed of the long-awaited arrival of Israel's Messiah King, in response to which, readers are told, they made their way westward in search of the child (2:1-2).

But Israel already had a king, reasoned a nervous Herod (v. 3), who then sought to interfere with the new One's coming (vv. 4-12). He inquired of the visitors under the guise of wanting to worship the new king himself (v. 8). Being wise men, they perceived his malice and departed the region after briefly visiting the two-year-old child themselves (v. 12). Grand upheaval associated with Herod's ill will was then developed in 2:1-12, and vv. 16-18, activity that prompted Joseph and Mary to make haste out of Israel, in 13-16, until word of Herod's death allowed them to return and settle in Nazareth (vv. 19-23).

Though Matthew told the early childhood story, the virginal Mary is marginal for his purposes—though not so with Luke later. That so little attention is given to Mary raises the question as to why she should be the object of adoration. Matthew developed the marriage and birthing story, true; but, *his focus of Divine attention was on Joseph* (whom the angel visited and spoke to), *and not on Mary.*

Woman By Divine Design

In Matthew's account, Mary seemed to play a small part and comes across as being more "swept up" into the story than a principal actor in the drama itself.

Moving along in the Text, Matthew noted the miracle of Peter's mother-in-law, in 8:14-15, and replicated Mark's stories of the woman with the flow of blood and Jairus' daughter in 9:18-26. Though Matthew followed Mark, he didn't just *follow* Mark. In 12:46-50, readers come upon something new: Jesus' "mother and brothers" were outside a residence seeking His attention. Someone told him, "Look, your mother and brothers are standing outside, wanting to speak with you" (v. 47). Jesus' response *seemed* to disrespect them all: "Anyone who does the will of my Father in Heaven is my brother and sister and mother" (v. 50). Sounds like He was saying: "What do they matter? You people are my real family."

We do not know the nature of their visit, though we do know the nature of some of the visitors: *we know that His brothers were not kindly disposed toward Jesus and were unbelievers* (cf. Jn. 7:1-5, esp. v. 5). Jesus' pointing to His followers as His family may well have been in response to that. Conjecture aside, there is no reason to think that He left them outside, much as we shouldn't read too much into this and conclude that Jesus disrespected His mother.

Was Jesus disrespecting His mother? We think not, and prefer envisioning this as a story that underscores that Believers become part of the new "family of God." It's a

Jesus and Women – Matthew's Gospel

great point. However, a mother who was indeed worthy of disrespect did make her way into the narrative.

Matthew went on to tell how John the Baptist was imprisoned by Herod the Tetrarch (14:1, 3) and that he was eventually beheaded at the behest of Herod's unethically acquired wife, Herodias. John dared publicly condemn the illicitly acquired union. Herodias was already wed to Herod's brother Philip (v. 3-4); Herod, however, took her from him—an arrangement that she seemed to prefer. Matthew didn't give an inordinate amount of particulars (Luke gave more); he did note, however, that she put up her daughter (whom the historian Josephus identifies as Salomé) to the task of arousing Herod at his birthday party (v. 6), in response to which the excited man promised Salomé whatever she wanted (v. 7).

Expectations that birthday boys usually get what they want at their parties aside, here, at her mother's urging (v. 8), Salomé pressed for something that Herod didn't want, but that Herodias did: John's death (v. 8). John the Baptist was summarily executed and his head was brought in on a platter (v. 11)—all at the urging of a seductive girl and a manipulating wife. This incident, among others, serves notice that women can just about always use sexual arousal to manipulate males and that, thus inclined and reclined, men can, will, and do go against their better judgment to satisfy a seductive woman's bidding.

Not long after this mother-and-daughter story was told, Matthew picked up on another of Mark's stories—with another addendum. As in Mark 7:24-30, the story of Jesus and the Syro-Phoenician woman's petitioning Jesus for her demented daughter reappears in Matt. 15:21-28. Mark was content to end with Jesus saying to the woman, "Go your way, the devil has gone out of your daughter" (Mk. 7:29). But Matthew put more emotion in the moment, adding to Mark's blander notation, "Jesus answered her, *'O woman, great is your faith!'*...and her daughter was made whole from that very hour" (authors' emphasis; 15:28). Apparently, a marginalized woman—and a gentile at that—had faith-power to move a mountain. For her, strength did not come exclusively from a male—though women can, do, and should draw strength from men; rather, *she had a faith through which she, herself, could get the better of the day's trouble!* Would that others did likewise!

The replication of Mark's stories is further noted in 19:1-10, where the question of divorce was brought up. As with the others, the Text follows the lead of Mark's rendition, which it no doubt employs (cf. Mk. 10:1-12), but it adds the male disciples' odd-sounding, collective response. In the wake of Jesus' saying that marriage should be binding, and that casual divorcement should be eschewed outright (Matt. 19:4-9), the men express alarm and ask why then marry? Matthew quotes them: "The disciples said to Him, 'If this is the situation between a husband and wife, it is better not to marry'" (v. 10).

This is a strange response. But the women-related stories are already showing themselves to be odd, so why expect

Jesus and Women – Matthew's Gospel

any difference here?

At face value, the men seem to be saying, in effect, "Gee, if a man can't get rid of his wife on a whim and exchange her for something newer, younger, or different, and do it for any reason whatsoever (as was the day's standard), then why bother taking a wife in the first place!?"

OK, guys.... What are these idiots asking and what are they saying about themselves by asking it?

We do well to stop and come to terms with how stupid this question is! This, in fact, may well be the dumbest comment in all of biblical literature!

Though we are unsure exactly what those morons were actually thinking, we can observe that Jesus *graciously* followed in v. 11 by stating, "Not everyone can accept this saying." He further noted that some men need not negotiate with the opposite sex, their being castrated "eunuchs" (v. 12a). For the rest of men, however, being sexual men—not being castrated sorts and thus possessing sexual appetites and all that goes with those impulses— He says: "He who is able to accept this, let him accept it" (v. 12b). But what does Jesus mean by that, exactly? Here is what we understand Jesus to be saying: *There is not to be sexual contact without a contract;* and *that contract is to be binding* in perpetuity between the man and the woman. This is the standard. If men don't want to "play by the rules, they ought not to play with the women." Jesus says, in effect, "If you are not wiling to abide by this principle, castrate yourselves and join the eunuchs."

After discussing eunuchs, Matthew followed with a variety of *wedding/marriage scorn* stories.

In 22:1ff., the Kingdom of God was likened to "a king who arranged a wedding for his son," who then experienced the reality that disinterested guests were not willing to come (v. 3) and acted shamefully in the process of rejecting his repeated offers (vv. 4-7). Some refused to come; others tried to sneak in uninvited and ill prepared: they attempted to enter "without a wedding garment" (v. 11), but were subsequently "bound...and thrown into the outer darkness" (v. 13).

Eventually following this was another shameful marriage-scorn story. One would expect loyal girlfriends to make the necessary provisions to participate in their friend's wedding. Not so in the following story. In the case of the "Ten Virgins," in 25:1-13, half of the women proved indifferent to their friend's pending marriage. They betrayed decorum, didn't make the requisite provisions, and were found out when their lights were running out of oil. Anxiously scurrying about looking for oil, they were rebuffed by individual suppliers who said, Go get the oil yourself; we are not going to give you a drop of ours (v. 9). The groom came, the wedding went off without a hitch, and those prepared went to the celebration. Later, the others came, wanted entrance, and were pushy about it (v. 11). The bridegroom pushed right back, however,

Jesus and Women – Matthew's Gospel

saying, "I don't know you!" (v. 12); in effect, beat it, you're not on the guest list!

These wedding-scorn stories have obvious soteriological (salvation) and eschatological (End Times) implications. As for the former, individuals need to respond to the invitation to be "saved;" as for the latter, those who do not respond in the affirmative while the "offer is on the table," will later wish they had when they experience the results of their self-inflicted exclusion from the Marriage Supper of the Lamb. These important points aside, that the whole business is framed in institutional love language presumed that Jewish readers would know that (1) women are to be cherished, (2) marriage partners are to be honored and their union is to be upheld, (3) weddings are to be celebrated, and (4) violations of the above are contrary to nature—an offense to God's design!—and are to be abhorred.

Like Mark, Matthew concludes with a "First Fruits" story—an "Easter" story—where the Marys are depicted as central to the Resurrection story (28:1-10). The only man shining on Resurrection Sunday morning is the glowing Jesus! Beyond His rise, the story is punctuated by the male disciples' lackluster performances, which are counterbalanced by the women's: *the women stood by Jesus and were the first to acknowledge that He had risen.*

So, what does a review of the women-related stories in Mark and Matthew reveal? In sum, we observe that, in terms of volume, the first Gospels are rather lean on women's stories. Nevertheless, the few passages that do reflect interaction are informative. We will see that Luke's Gospel augments the limitations found in the first two Gospels. Luke's rendition contributes much, much more about women; and to his story we will now attend.

Jesus and Women – Luke's Gospel

Jesus and Women in Luke's Gospel

The earliest Gospel, Mark, said nothing about the young Jesus. Matthew's Gospel contained insightful infancy narrative on Him and highlighted *some* women's issues—at least more than Mark's. Still, Matthew's had lean pickings and, even when dealing with the birth narrative, the emphasis in Matthew's Gospel was on Joseph, *not* Mary. Matthew told that Joseph was visited by an angel and was directed by the messenger (Matt. 1:20-21); that's it. By contrast, and while commenting on the very same basic story, *Luke informed that Mary, herself, was likewise visited by that angel (Luke identifies him as Gabriel), and that a conversation between Gabriel and her ensued.* In 1:26-28, readers are told that the angel Gabriel was sent by God to a virgin betrothed and, having come in, the angel said to her, "Rejoice highly favored one, the Lord is with you!" When it came to bringing Jesus into the world, Mary wasn't simply a backdrop to the story, neither was she a non-person or passive damsel being acted upon by forces beyond her control and absent her participation. She factors more significantly in this Gospel, as do other women, and for reasons that will be made apparent later.

In vv. 39-45, Mary visited her pregnant relative Elizabeth—the mother of John the Baptist, soon to be born. No other writers were interested in this story. Luke was, however, and he described it as follows: "It happened that...Elizabeth was filled with the Holy Spirit. Then she spoke out with a loud voice and said, 'Blessed are you among women!'" This was followed by a rather long anthem

Woman By Divine Design

in which Mary went on record with some prophetic unction of her own (vv. 46-55).

While it is interesting that God was depicted as visiting and interacting with a woman (Gabriel's visit), or that women visited each other (Mary and Elizabeth), more significantly, *women are capable of prophesying under the unction of the Holy Spirit*, saying things both to and about women. Luke further quoted Elizabeth's prophecy: "blessed is *she* who believed" (v. 45). He then drew attention to Mary, who countered with inspired verbiage of her own: God has visited the lowly state of *His maidservant* (v. 48) and: He who is mighty has done great things *for me* (v. 49).

Mary's response gives us insight. She probably was perceived by others as something of a "loose woman," one who brought shame to herself, her family, and to her good husband, Joseph. What a horrible feeling it must have been to be the object of scorn and derision, to know that people were looking at and pre-judging her. To her credit, Mary seemed to bear it all very gracefully.

Luke's employment of gender-inclusive verbiage here—and elsewhere in his Gospel and in Acts—is significant and opens up a whole new and important women-friendly dynamic worth exploring. Before pressing ahead with such exploration, however, let's attend to the Text some more, and note how we are *not* simply trying to build a big case on a small and essentially baseless foundation.

Jesus and Women – Luke's Gospel

In addition to noting that women were themselves hearing from God and speaking about Him, Luke also drew attention to the disheartening disrespect that the pregnant Mary experienced, with "no room in the inn" being made available for her (2:1-7). Even unregenerate men who have little interest in women beyond using them to satisfy their pleasures know to give way to a pregnant woman in late term—to open a door, to give up a seat on the bus, or whatever. That Mary got no such treatment is interesting, especially the contrast that even as she was being publicly disrespected, God was raising her estate in life.

Mark provided no infancy narrative. Matthew developed one, but highlighted the man (Joseph), "wise men" visiting Israel, and a wicked man (Herod) bent on thwarting the arrival of a King-man—Jesus. These, coupled with the attendant, subsequent social and political disruptions, which prompted Joseph to take his family to Egypt, punctuated the story. Matthew's Christmas story was a story about men. Not so with Luke. He didn't contradict Matthew, but he did nuance it differently by bringing in other, women-related stories.

Luke's infancy narrative avoids all of the tumult and confusion associated with Jesus' birth in Matthew. In Luke, the royal family isn't left running for their lives, and there is not a word about the slaughter of the innocent children in Bethlehem. Luke finished his reasonably placid infancy story noting that a prophetess named Anna bore

Woman By Divine Design

witness to Jesus in Jerusalem: "And there was one, Anna, a prophetess, the daughter of Phanuel... [and she] served God with fastings and prayers night and day. [Seeing Jesus] she gave thanks unto the Lord, and spoke of Him to all those who looked for redemption in Israel" (2:36-38). As with Elizabeth and Mary before her, Luke gives word here of another woman prophesying.

Over and again from its very beginning, *Luke's Gospel confronts readers with the fact that—like it or not—God personally visits women and can be heard speaking through them!* Luke, an associate of Paul, was given to demonstrating that women were more socially and spiritually empowered in the new "Christian" economy, than before. Luke gave readers more stories—stories found *only* in Luke—where women are the principal actors in the dramas, the heroines around whom the morals of the stories unfold.

It is from Luke, for example, that we learn of Jesus' love for the widow at Nain (7:11-17). Despite there being a large and pressing crowd (v. 11), Jesus was represented as stopping what He was doing to go attend to a desperate, male-less woman—a widow who had just lost her only son (v. 12). Luke said: "When the Lord saw her He felt compassion for her, and said to her, 'Do not weep'" (v. 13). He then opened the coffin and spoke to the young man who subsequently arose (vv. 14-15). This miracle isn't just any miracle, for it expresses the interest of One given to coming to the aid of a needy woman—a virtue evidenced over and again in the Text.

Jesus and Women – Luke's Gospel

In Luke's Gospel, Jesus didn't help just "good girls"; He helped "bad" ones too. The Widow of Nain parable is followed by mention of John the Baptist's imprisonment. We noted in our discussion of Matthew 14 that John's death came on the heels of a lusty woman's bidding. Luke followed his information about John with a different story altogether: Luke didn't tell of a woman who used sex to do bad; rather, he told of a woman who used to use sex, but repented and possibly became one of Jesus' loyal followers and supporters. This is likely no mere coincidence.

The story starts off well enough, with Jesus asked to dine at a Pharisee's house (7:36). What might have otherwise been a story of Jesus making headway with a friendly Jewish leader (as with Nicodemus in Jn. 3), took on a rather odd twist. Luke informed that the engagement was abruptly and rudely interrupted by "a woman in the city who was a sinner" (v. 37; cf., v. 39). Her being a "sinner" is perceived as a lightly veiled reference to her practicing "the world's oldest profession"—prostitution. This woman is said to have entered uninvited carrying expensive perfume in an alabaster jar and started expressing devotion to Jesus: she "began to wash His feet with her tears, and wipe them with the hairs of her head; and kissed His feet, and anointed them" (vv. 38-39). The religious leaders expressed shock and disbelief, both by her breach of decorum and the apparent fact that Jesus—a prophet—didn't seem to know what sort of woman this was. He did know though; but, He was less interested in what she *was* than what she *was becoming* by virtue of her repentance.

Woman By Divine Design

In vv. 47-48, Jesus declared that she was "forgiven," and told her to "go in peace" in v. 50. It is possible that she didn't go away, but rather joined the group and became one of Jesus' loyal followers.

In 8:1-3, Luke went on to inform that the apostolic troupe was traveling about and ministering. Beyond mentioning that "the twelve were with Him" in v. 1, Luke noted that "certain women" were also traveling with them, and that these women were "helping to support them from their own means" (v. 2a and 3b). Luke mentioned three women by name, but said there were "many" others (v. 3).

"Mary Magdalene, from whom He had cast out seven demons," was noted first, then Joanna the wife of Chuza (Herod's steward), and Susanna.

That these women had "their own means" indicates that they belonged to a higher social class than even the Apostles, among whom were several fishermen, a tax collector, and a couple of revolutionary zealots.

The reference to Joanna being the wife of Herod's steward tells us a lot.

If one considers that "stewards" were well-placed, MBA-type business managers, and that Herod's household represented the richest and most powerful dynasty in Israel at the time, one is left with the impression that this was a woman of considerable financial means.

Jesus and Women – Luke's Gospel

Absent Jesus-related resolutions within these women, one would *not* expect Joanna and other "women of means" to have anything whatsoever to do with lepers, prostitutes, and social outcasts, given their being polar opposites, socially. Nevertheless, *all* of Jesus' followers recognized that their base natures required redemption and they worked together to support Jesus in bringing others to that realization. Without the unifying message of Jesus, the women who financially supported His ministry likely would have disdained the outcasts of society with whom His ministry brought them into contact. Without Jesus' message, lowly followers who had been "changed" by Jesus might have resented their wealthier patrons as "holier than thou." We don't want to let our imaginations read more into the Text than is actually there; but the contrasts are indeed striking and attest to the fact that individuals who can be estranged from one another, and from God, can find forgiveness from both, through Jesus, and begin life afresh as friends and fellow workers for the Kingdom.

In 13:10-17, Jesus happened upon another woman. She wasn't a "streetwalker"; she wasn't even a "walker"—for she'd been crippled for the better part of eighteen years. She was notably "bent double" and, as a result, "was unable to stand up straight." Jesus saw her and "He laid His hands upon her, and immediately she was made straight" (vv. 11-13). This miracle invoked the ire of religious people, who construed His performing the miracle on the Sabbath as problematic (v. 14). Jesus' response "shamed" them,

Woman By Divine Design

however (v. 17a). *His interlocutors gave no thought to the woman*, and only saw the alleged violation; Jesus, by contrast, cared for the woman: "Hypocrites!" said He. "Ought not this woman, being a daughter of Abraham… be loosed from this bond?" (vv. 15-16)

While this and other miracles prove Jesus' divinity, evidenced by His being able to master the laws of nature at His beckoning, this miracle, in like manner, attests to an aspect of His Divine/humanity, too: *He didn't just care about proving who He is; He cared for women!*

He seemed to care about big and little issues alike.

No doubt, many a housewife can relate to a woman's pressing her fingers through her couch's cushions in search of a lost ring or a coin. It's for this reason, perhaps, that Jesus is on record in the world before luxury couches with the parable of the Lost Coin, wherein Luke depicted an anxious woman searching her home for one of her silver coins (15:8-10). This story, culled from women's experience, becomes a model for repentance; for "when she has found it," said Jesus, "she calls her friends… saying I found the piece which was lost. Likewise, I say to you, there is joy in the presence of the angels of God over one sinner who repents" (v. 10). This story would have resonated with women particularly—as would the others.

The womanly "Lost Coin" parable was immediately followed by the manly "Prodigal Son" story in 15:11-32. While granting that a sentimental father is given to

Jesus and Women – Luke's Gospel

welcoming his wayward son back home (vv. 20-24), the Text says more about the angst of his older son, who resented the returning brother's preferential treatment. Unlike the previous housewife parable, this one is as much about dealing with the heartless and competitive male's temper as it is a story of God's Grace at work in the world (vv. 25-32).

A few parables later, Luke put both a man and woman in the same story—with the man looking like a fool for ignoring the pleas of a vulnerable woman.

"There was in a certain city a judge who did not fear God nor regard man. Now there was a widow in that city, and she came to him, saying, 'Get justice for me from my adversary.' And he would not...yet he said to himself, 'because this widow keeps bothering me, I will avenge her lest by her continual coming she weary me'" (18:1-5). Jesus made her continual petitioning an example of prevailing prayer, saying: "And shall God not avenge His own elect who cry out day and night to Him?" (v. 7)

This story is fascinating for a variety of reasons.

On the one hand, it plays into the tendency of males to complain that women relentlessly "nag" them and use incessant petitions to wear them down. But, Jesus calls the woman's action a virtue that God responds to, *vindicating the woman for her persistence* and suggesting that the disciples should adopt the practice. In the parable, the unjust male finally relented and gave the petitioner the justice she deserved—the justice she should not have had to press him for in the first place. Here, again, is a story *written from a woman's perspective and designed to speak to, for, and about women.* It is not just about the principle, important as the principle is.

Luke and others told us that many jeered Jesus at the end. Luke informed, as well, that female disciples attended Him until the end (23:27b) and that, while carrying His cross to Golgotha, Jesus turned and gave a prophetic word to the "daughters of Jerusalem" (vv. 28-31)—evidence that He thought of them, even at the end.

Women factor significantly in Luke's Gospel; and an examination of the Text gives the impression that there are liberating implications for women. That Luke wrote his Gospel to complement and defend Paul's ministry is telling. As we shall see later, more than anyone, it was Paul who advocated that God has done something new in the world and that, through the Church, somehow the distinctions between males and females—as with others—are rendered less significant. We will get to Paul later. In summing up Luke, at this juncture we do well to note this, as we consider Luke's to be a very liberating and female-friendly accounting of what Jesus said and did.

Jesus and Women – John's Gospel

Jesus and Women in John's Gospel

Unlike Luke and Matthew—and much like Mark—John paid no attention whatsoever to Jesus' early years. The Church's inventory of Christmas Text comes from the former writers and not from the latter. While Luke seemed particularly keen on Jesus' humanity and on attendant ancillary family matters, John focused on Jesus' divinity.

In chapter two, John placed Jesus and Mary at a wedding celebration. The beverages were nearly depleted and, concerned that the guests might get slighted, Mary went on record expressing concern to Jesus over the matter (v. 3). In response to her saying "They have no wine," Jesus said, "Woman, what does your concern have to do with me?" (v. 4)

At the risk of sounding like a scolding Yiddish grandmother, and for rhetorical purposes, we ask the following: Is this any way for a son to talk to his mother—never mind the way the Son of God should talk to His mother?

Let's see.

Was Jesus snapping at His mother?

The disparaging-sounding term "woman" could also be read: "*Madam*"—a respectful term; and the follow-up to it could just be a way of saying: "Madam, *that's your responsibility!*" Should that reading prevail, Jesus' response could just as easily be read as an empowering retort as a disrespectful one. That Mary immediately ordered the servants to attend to Jesus' wishes argues for empowerment and casts her in the role of a supervisor, affording her some command presence that should not be minimized (2:5). What may seem like a disempowering story may well reveal power. As we shall see, women are *not* minimized and disrespected in John's Gospel.

After going "toe to toe" with a member of Judaism's religious elite in chapter three, in chapter four Jesus is on the road to the Galilee (v. 3), by way of Samaria (v. 4). There, He happened upon a woman at a well with whom He struck up a very interesting and engaging conversation (4:7-38).

In the rather spirited dialogue, Jesus gently confronted her over her less-than-desirable string of sexual relationships (vv. 16-18). Jesus proved to be so insightful and prophetic that the conversation resulted in her perceiving that He was not an ordinary man. She said, "Sir, I perceive that you are a prophet" (v. 19). The "Prophet" then expressed to her the imperative to "worship God in spirit and in truth" (vv. 21-24), after which He flatly confessed that He is the long-awaited "Messiah" (vv. 25-26).

This very personal and revealing dialogue comes across in a manner that is comfortable and natural. Therein, a comfortable Jesus is given to doing His Father's work and to disclosing to her—a Samaritan woman—all sorts of truths.

Jesus and Women – John's Gospel

When the male disciples returned from running their designated errand, they were troubled by the casual interaction, and wondered "Why are you talking with her"—that woman!? (v. 27). John noted their displeasure, but didn't make much of it. Worth noting, for our purposes here though, is that Jesus wasn't the least bit disconcerted; in fact, He used the interaction as a springboard to exhort the men to reach beyond their class, their gender bias, and their comfort zones generally, and not to differentiate, doing well to apply themselves to the greater harvest (vv. 27-38). Jesus' comfortable conversation with the Samaritan woman stands in marked contrast to the tenser one with Nicodemus in the preceding chapter. The discomfort of His disciples is telling too, and further underscores that Jesus had no problem interacting with women—or any group—a tendency that prompted some to wrongfully accuse Him of being "a little too friendly with the ladies," elsewhere. (Matt 11:18-19, Luke 15:2)

Later, John told how the sisters Martha and Mary sent word to their friend Jesus that their brother was ill (11:1-3). John informs his readers that "Jesus loved Martha and Mary" (v. 5). Still, much as Jesus seemed previously to give a cool response to His own mother at a wedding reception (see 2:4, above), so, too, He gave a rather cool response here, opting not to attend to Lazarus at that time (v. 6), and letting him slip off into death as a result (v. 14). After waiting awhile, Jesus finally arrived and found that Lazarus had already been dead for four days and was entombed (v. 38-39)—and Jesus intentionally missed all of it.

Woman By Divine Design

After revealing to Martha that "I am the resurrection and the life. He who believes in Me though he may die he shall live" (v. 25a), Jesus went off to prove the point. Out came Lazarus in v. 44; and out came supper in the following chapter—thanks to Martha and Mary. That Jesus' explicit telling of His resurrection came out of a conversation with a woman is itself telling and reflects the comfort He felt when dealing with women. That women responded kindly to Him seems only natural.

"Then... Jesus came to Bethany, where Lazarus was who had been dead. There they made Him a supper; and Martha served... Mary took a pound of very costly oil and spikenard, anointed the feet of Jesus, and wiped His feet with her hair" (12:1-3). In response to Judas' snarling and deceitful consternation over the woman's sacrifice, Jesus rebuked him and defended her, saying flatly, "Leave her alone" (v. 7a). Jesus' defense of her is telling, is it not?

John was keen on noting that women were some of Jesus' most loyal supporters. Jesus recognized their support and responded in kind. John went on to attest that Jesus was abandoned, outright, by the male Apostles. He informed, though, that "there stood by the cross of Jesus His mother, and His mother's sister, Mary the wife of Clopas, and Mary Magdalene" (19:25) and that Jesus had the presence of mind to commend His mother into John's custody just before the last breath at His dying moment (v. 27). As did the other writers, John noted that the women not only attended to Him at the cross, but that

Jesus and Women – John's Gospel

they frequented the tomb where He was later deposited and from whence He rose—their being the first witnesses to that effect (20:1ff.).

A few comments on female loyalty are worth noting here. That mothers can, will, and do die for their children is without question. Carrying a child creates a bond that often becomes inseparable, extending beyond the physical separation at birth. Maternal instinct explains why Mary stood by her beloved Son to the end. That other women did so, as well, points to an innate sense of loyalty that seemed more characteristic of the females than the males.

Jesus and Women - Summary

Summary: Jesus and Women in the Gospels

So what does one glean from a cursory assessment of the Gospels' treatment of women?

For openers, we note that there isn't a lot of attention given to women in the Gospel writings. Need this be problematic? We, the authors, think not. John explicitly voices his Gospel's purpose as assisting folk to "believe that Jesus is the Christ, the Son of God, and that by believing you may have life in His name" (Jn. 20:31). Because we can safely assume that the other writers had similar intents, the dearth of women-related material should come as no surprise: it simply wasn't a principal concern.

Though the Gospel writers weren't primarily concerned with women's matters, they do demonstrate that Jesus was concerned with women's welfare. *Everything* Jesus said and did is timeless—including what concerned women. His attitudes and actions can, and should, be applied to all generations.

In the Gospel traditions, women are shown to be respected by Jesus, deeply valued by Him, and much appreciated.

Paul and Women
Introduction
Some pulpit-pounding, ranting reverends advocate that "their people" should keep "their women" under control! When asked to give a theological accounting for this position, they respond: "It is in the Bible!" Is it really?

Some years back, a cartoon appeared depicting Paul arriving by boat on a distant and foreign island. When word got out of his arrival, a throng of irate women assembled to protest his presence. The mounting tensions cascaded upward and couldn't be bottled up. A mob scene was in the making. Outraged, some women abandoned lady-like decorum and were heard screaming at the top of their lungs, while others were seen spending their boundless energies pacing back and forth, flinging banners reading "Unfair to Women," "Paul is a Male Chauvinist Pig" and worse. Disconcerted as they all were, some did both—and with reckless abandon. Paul is depicted as looking rather sheepishly at the crowd, and chuckling, "Heh, heh, I see you girls got my letters!"

Such is the perception. But is it warranted? In the cartoon's case, it might be that they "received his biblical letters," but did they really understand them? Did they really "get" them?

In his book *Freedom in the Ancient World*, Dr. Herbert Muller opined that they did: "Although they [women] fared well with Jesus...," said he, "their denigration began with St. Paul."[3] Was he correct? Paul is universally understood to be the one who offered the Christian context for the discrediting, disparaging, and the dehumanizing of womankind.

Muller's critique aside, and that unfavorable label notwithstanding, we do well to think for ourselves and wonder to what extent Paul was actually culpable.

Paul is credited with writing thirteen epistles. They appear in our Bibles from longest to shortest: Romans has sixteen chapters; 1 Corinthians has sixteen chapters and 2 Corinthians has thirteen; Galatians has six chapters; Ephesians has six chapters; Philippians has four chapters; Colossians has four chapters; 1 Thessalonians has five chapters and 2 Thessalonians has three; 1 Timothy has six chapters, whereas 2 Timothy has four; Titus has three; and Philemon finishes the collection with but one. All in all, bulk-wise, Paul brings thirteen books to the New Testament's collection, totaling eighty-seven chapters. In my English Bible, the Pauline chapters take up forty-eight pages out of eight hundred and sixty-three, for both Old and New Testaments. Everything Paul actually wrote about women could perhaps be squeezed on one of those pages—amounting to a little more than two percent of

Paul and Women - Introduction

his writings. The scant attention to women gives rise to the question of whether women-related issues were even a major consideration for Paul. Were he to have been hell-bent on putting women in their places, as is alleged, it would seem he'd have given more attention to doing so.

In the interest of tendering a responsible answer to the question of what Paul really said about women, we will offer: (1) a representation of the order in which Paul wrote his correspondence, and (2) a reasonably fresh consideration of (a) what the Apostle said about women and (b) the context within which he said it. Let's read his own words and see if we can vindicate Paul from the critics' den and get a view of God's "Divine design" for women as a result.

Paul and Women - Galatians

Galatians

Written in about 49AD (after Paul's first missionary journey), Galatians gives readers a window into Paul's thought world and helps readers get at its essence.

In his own words, Paul's unique message for humanity was given him by direct revelation from God (1:11-12), and wasn't simply handed down from the other Apostles (1:14-24). Paul informed that at the center of his divinely "revealed" theology was a rearrangement of social structuring, an extension of a kindness and Grace that God was now extending to all of His creation through His Son the Messiah (3:1-5:12). Central to him was the conviction that: "There is [now] neither Jew nor Greek, there is neither slave nor free, there is neither male nor female; for you are all one in Christ" (3:28; cf. Col. 3:11). Paul finished his letter with an exhortation to walk in that loving and Grace-disposed Spirit (5:13-24), to practice love (5:25-6:5), to be gracious (6:6-10), and not to be shaken by adversaries (6:11-18).

Given that there are biological differences between males and females, we do well to consider what he meant by noting that the differences have somehow collapsed and that the sexes are now "one." He didn't tell us specifically in the aforementioned quote, but the natural outgrowth of this conviction surfaces in his other writings, as we shall see.

Paul and Women - Thessalonians

1 and 2 Thessalonians

Not long after penning the Galatian document, in 50-51AD Paul wrote his Thessalonian correspondences. In 1 Thess. 4:3-8, when Paul addressed the whole congregation he firmly asserted the need for the men to "abstain from sexual immorality" (v. 3), to see to it that men take wives "honorably" (v. 4) and not "defraud" a brother (arguably the bride's family) by failing to do so properly (v. 6). He then followed with a brief exhortation toward "brotherly love" in vv. 9-12. Closing in 5:12, Paul recommended that the brethren "recognize those who labor among you," but he mentioned nobody by name.[4]

Though Paul mentioned women in this letter, he seemed principally interested in men's conduct in relation to women more than in women themselves. At issue was the imperative for men to position themselves properly toward the opposite sex, and not to let unbridled impulses get the better of them. Paul is thus observed requiring that men respect women.

In his follow-up letter, Paul was preoccupied with eschatology—Bible prophecy. In 1 Thess. 4:13-18, he had mentioned the Messiah's second coming; in his second letter to the Thessalonians, he picked up on prophetic matters and went into detail about the antiChrist's appearance and rule, and his eventual displacement at Christ's second coming (2:3-15).

Concerned as he was about the end of the world, Paul was not as given to issues associated with living in this one.

Woman By Divine Design

Women's issues are indirectly addressed here by Paul's instruction that men be industrious financially and provide for their households (3:6-14). Again, as with the previous writings, what Paul wrote seems to have been principally aimed at and about men and *not* women.

Paul and Women - Corinthians

1 and 2 Corinthians

Paul's Corinthian correspondences followed in 55 AD and 56 AD and were written while he was on his third missionary journey. While a comprehensive unpacking of these fascinating Corinthian writings goes beyond the scope of this volume, some detailing is warranted here, given the depth and breadth of women-related issues dealt with herein.

After Paul left Corinth, an official delegation sent from a well-respected female patron named "Chloe" (1 Cor. 1:11), comprising Stephanas, Fortunatus, and Achaicus (16:17), made haste to catch up to their spiritual father, Paul. The befuddled messengers gave voice to a host of grave concerns in the interest of securing their beloved patriarch's advice. Hoping to solve some problems and assuage their aggravation, in 1:10-6:20 Paul responded to their verbal reports.

On the basis of their communications, Paul tackled "divisions" within the Church around personalities (1:10-4:21)—spirited along by false teachers, given to usurping Paul's apostolic authority. This was a real problem for Paul—and one arguably related to spirited female preachers with whom Paul was at odds (see below).

After discussing the divisions at length, Paul took on a case of severe sexual impropriety where a young man took advantage of his young stepmother in his father's absence (5:1-13). Paul likewise dealt with Church infighting and concomitant lawsuits (6:1-8); he finished with a follow-up to 5:1-13 above, by exhorting the Corinthians toward moral purity in 6:9-20. In 7:2-16:9, Paul began working through issues in the letter sent him, which was subsequently hand-delivered to him (cf. 7:1).

By way of response, Paul began by taking up and legitimizing sexual relations between the sexes in 7:1-40. Though he preferred no sexual contact absent a marriage contract, he had nothing disparaging to say about sexual contact in and of itself—as some apparently did. Paul legitimized marriage as the context within which lovemaking was to be experienced—no exceptions. In 11:1-16, Paul weighed in more on the relationship between the sexes. In this case, however, marriage mattered only insofar as the male-female interrelationship served as a model to order Church conduct. At issue here was women giving prophetic voice to spiritual matters in religious services. Contrary to the prevailing Jewish custom, Paul seemed content with the practice of women giving prophetic exhortations—provided that their doing so was employed within delineated parameters. He didn't want ecstatic utterances *without translations* distracting from the main activity, and thus he provided standards for men and women alike.

One can only assume that, with his close associate Luke, Paul saw both "sons and *daughters* prophesying" as an authenticating experience, one identified with Pentecost itself (Acts 2:1ff., esp. vv. 14, 17-18). *Though Paul was an intellectual, there seems to have been room for ecstatic utterance in his mind, practice, and churches.* The Church

Paul and Women - Corinthians

"body" was said by him in chapter 12 to be quite diverse, and being multifaceted, provides room for everyone in it. Assuming that women's prophetic and ecstatic unctions—noted previously in chapter 11—were interpreted for all to hear and benefit from, and not just some sort of show of an alleged superior spirituality (which it is not!), Paul seemed pleased to allow for them; should the verbiage not be interpreted, however, Paul scorned the practice outright as not helpful, and a practice needing to be abandoned (14:1-40; cf. 11:1ff.). This he did *not* because of its being women's talk (which seems to be the case based on chapter 11), but because the ecstatic verbiage itself comes without the benefit of a translation that can make it meaningful for all the women and men present.

Throughout chapter 14, Paul was countering false teachers given to celebrating how spiritual they were, evidenced by their alleged spiritual giftedness. Paul's troubling comments in 14:34-40 need to be understood against this backdrop and in this light. Therein, and by way of response to the above, he said: "Let your women be silent in the churches, for they are not permitted to speak; but they are to be submissive as the law says. And if they want to learn something, let them ask their husbands at home; for it is shameful for women to speak in church... Let all things be done decently and in order." Within the ebb and flow of his argument, at issue here seems to have been some Corinthian women's unaccompanied prophetic utterances. Taking the lead from this, some argue that women should not speak in church at all, in any context—period! This seems an unnecessary

Woman By Divine Design

assumption; for, in this case, Paul was principally dealing with the matter of ecstatic utterances. [Editor's Note: Jeff's forthcoming book, in which he will follow Paul's footsteps through Turkey and Greece, will also explore the customs of women and teaching and learning in Paul's time.]

As he closed 1 Corinthians, Paul commended the famous teacher Apollos (16:12), the faithfulness of the "household of Stephanas" (vv. 15-18), and then finished by drawing attention to the husband and wife teaching team of Aquila and Priscilla (v. 19). Those minded to argue that a woman's voice has no place in Christian education, period, would do well to note Luke's testimony that one of the day's premiere educators (Apollos) was himself tutored by Aquila *and Priscilla*. In Acts 18:24-28, Luke says in v. 26, "they [Aquila and Priscilla] took him [Apollos] aside and explained to him the way of God more accurately." Worth noting is Luke's mentioning the woman first, in v. 18. Because Luke was the expositor of Paul, *this seems evidence enough that women's perspective and voices were, in fact, appreciated by the Apostle Paul.* Today, there is not a single male pastor, worth his salt, who does not realize that, were it not for an influential wife or girlfriend, many men would not come to church—period.

Moving on, in 2 Corinthians, Paul reaffirmed his relationship with the Corinthian community which, by the time of that writing, was on better footing with him—likely because the pushy prophetesses who were undermining his authority lost some clout. Heartfelt reflections were shared in 1:3-

Paul and Women - Corinthians

7:16. Evidence that things had quieted down was further noted by the fact that Paul was confident enough to take a missions offering in chapters 8 and 9. In 10:1-13:10, Paul closes by "taking on" his detractors—the false teachers, noted above.

Reminding that he will "punish disobedience" (10:6; cf. vv. 1-6), Paul reasserts his paternal claim by drawing attention to his authority to teach and legislate affairs in Corinth (10: 7-13:10). In 11:5, Paul insists, "I am not at all inferior to these most eminent apostles" whom some of you mistakenly respect—a reference to the false teachers. He picked up on this shortly thereafter, saying: "in nothing am I behind the most eminent apostles... Truly the signs of an Apostle were accomplished among you... in signs and wonders and mighty deeds" (12:11-12). Paul's point was simple: don't be overly impressed by those super-spiritual sorts—likely some prophetess-types; they don't have anything over me. I have gifts too, despite the fact that I do most of my work using common language, while they attempt to impress you with their allegedly spiritual jargon and undermine my legitimate authority in the process of so doing.

Paul and Women - Romans

Romans

Paul wasn't nearly as intense when he wrote his Roman epistle in 57AD. Paul founded the Corinthian church, as he had those in Thessalonica and Galatia; however, he had never visited Rome and could only begin his letter by expressing his intention to do so at a later date (1:8-15), a point he closes on as well (15:22-33).

Let's look at what Paul says to the Romans concerning women.

In the wake of his taking up the matter of human sinfulness in Rom. 1:18-3:20, Paul underscored that Israel's Messiah has remedied the sin problem: faith in Him, says he, is humankind's answer (3:21-5:21). In 5:12, Paul noted that "through one man sin entered the world, and death through sin, and thus death spread to all men, because all sinned." He followed in v. 17 with "by one man's offense death reigned," forcing the conclusion that Paul believed that sin came into the world through a man—Adam. (At first, this might not seem like much; however, do keep it in mind, as readers will be asked to call upon this insight later.)

Paul brings up "sin" because he wants to inform that God has remedied the sin problem. Much as sin entered the human race because of Adam's sin, so too can righteousness be imputed because of another person's righteousness—Jesus'. After comparing and contrasting Adam and Jesus, Paul exhorts that followers of Jesus do well to leave aside the old, sinful ways and walk in the new ways (5:1-8:39). After a treatment of sinful Israel's past, present, and future (9:1-11:36), Paul gives his standard moral exhortations: be holy (12:1-2), serve others (12:3-8), be kindly disposed toward others and offer a good witness in this world (12:9-21), submit to legitimate, governmental authorities (13:1-7), and love others and keep your guard up (13:8-15:21). He closes by sharing his travel plans (15:22-33), after which he draws attention to a number of noteworthy individuals, twenty-six of whom he commends by name—many of them women.

In 16:1-2, the Apostle said: "I commend Phoebe our sister, who is a servant of the church in Cenchrea, that you may receive her in the Lord in a manner worthy of the saints, and assist her in whatever business she has need of you." Paul used the empowering Greek word *diakonon* to describe her, a word used later in Phil. 1:1; 1 Tim. 3:8, 10 and 12 to denote a "deacon." Paul not only commended her personally, but exhorted the men to make themselves available to assist her in her ministerial work.

In v. 3 he switches common order and betrays decorum in the process. Though previously referring to them as Aquila and Priscilla, he here says, "Greet Priscilla and Aquila, my fellow workers in Christ Jesus"—note the wife named first. He then notes Epaenetus and greets a Jewess named "Mary" ("Mariam" in Hebrew) in v. 6, followed by the husband and wife team of Andronicus and Junia, whom he refers to as "fellow prisoners" in v.

Paul and Women - Romans

7. Amplias is noted in v. 8, as are Urbanis and Stachys in v. 9, Apelles and the household of Aristobulus in v. 10, Herodian and Narcissus, in v. 11, Tryphena and Tryphosa and Persis in v. 12, finishing with Rufus and his mother in v. 13, Asyncritus, Phlegon, Hermas, Patrobas, Hermes in v. 14, and closing with Philologus and Julia, Nereus and his sister, and Olympas in v. 15.

Noteworthy in the listing is the noting of women. Would one bent on silencing women outright, period, commend Phoebe in vv. 1-2, Priscilla in v. 3, Mary in v. 6, Junia in v. 7, Tryphena and Tryphosa in v. 12, Persis in v. 12, Rufus' mother in v. 13, and Nereus' sister and Julia in v. 15? It seems hardly likely. Those bent on reading Paul as such would do well to take all of Paul's writings into consideration and not press for unmitigated female subservience on the basis of texts that are voided of their contexts.

Paul and Women - Philemon

Philemon

When Paul wrote to the Romans, he shared his travel plans, hoping to eventually visit them. He did make his way to Rome—not as he intended, but as a prisoner. While imprisoned in the imperial city, Paul wrote a postcard-like note to Philemon who lived in Colosse, in 61/62AD. At the same time that Paul wrote to the Church at Colosse (see Colossians below), he penned his brief note to Philemon, the owner of the home where the Church met.

Therein he expressed thanksgiving for Philemon (vv. 4-7) and offered a plea for a runaway slave of his, named Onesimus, whom Paul had befriended in Rome and who had subsequently converted under Paul's ministry. Paul wrote the letter on behalf of Onesimus. After addressing the reasonably wealthy Philemon, he then greeted the "beloved Apphia" and then an "Archippus" whom he refers to as a "fellow soldier" in v. 2. The "beloved Apphia" was Philemon's wife. As the "lady of the house"—and as such possessing standing in the "house church" by association—Paul addressed her affectionately, cordially, and personally, knowing that she would have superintended the day-to-day affairs of the servants, as was the custom of the lady of the house. Archippus was perhaps their son, who seemingly was given pastoral charge of the church meeting in their house (cf., Col. 4:17). In writing, Paul asks—insists!—that Philemon receive his former property now as a brother in Christ, and as an equal in Christ, not simply as runaway property (vv. 8-22), after which he closes (vv. 23-25).

Woman By Divine Design

The implications in all of this are many, reaching into aspects such as social order and the eradication of slavery. We will close with yet another aspect.

While commenting on the Galatian text, we were reminded of Paul's saying that, in Christ, "there is neither Jew nor Greek, there is neither slave nor free, there is neither male nor female; for you are all one in Christ" (3:28). Paul's adherence to this is amply demonstrated by his instructions to Philemon: that Philemon put aside the social structures that made his former slave Onesimus subservient to him, and perceive him now with realigned vision. This, coupled with the respect that Paul showed Apphia and women generally, lends credence to the proposition that Paul appreciated women's value and was given to lifting women up, not putting them down.

Paul and Women - Colossians

Colossians

This letter was written by Paul while he was imprisoned in Rome, in 61/62AD. It was hand-delivered by Tychicus and Onesimus, whom Paul dispatched for that very purpose (4:7-9). He opened with a standard salutation (1:1-2), followed by an expression of thanksgiving and prayer support (vv. 3-12). Wanting to combat a tendency to diminish Jesus' person and nature, Paul noted His preeminence over all in 1:13-2:23 and encouraged followers to live in a worthy manner, given that we bear His name. While pressing individuals to live rightly in a generally unrighteous world, Paul said we are to "*put off...* anger, wrath, malice, blasphemy [and] filthy language... [and to] *put on* the new man, who is renewed in knowledge according to the image of Him who created Him, where there is neither Greek nor Jew, circumcised nor uncircumcised, barbarian, Scythian, slave nor free" (3:8-11).

Unlike the Galatian Text noted previously (Gal. 3:28), this list of equals omits "neither male nor female." Perhaps this is because the expression can be misleading—for there certainly are differences between the sexes[5]—or perhaps it is because Paul followed with differentiating instructions. To the wives he said: "Wives, submit to your own husbands, as is fitting in the Lord," in v. 18; whereas, to the husbands, he said: "Husbands love your wives and do not be bitter toward them," in v. 19—themes he likewise took up in Ephesians, which follows. Implied in both cases is that women and men do well to keep their base impulses "in check," that we monitor our internal systems, and place a premium on *mutual subservience and the good of the other* when dealing with each other. This is Paul's point and it's a far cry from the depiction of him as the subjugator and destroyer of womankind.

Paul closed noting Tychicus and Onesimus, referenced previously (cf. 4:7, 9). Aristarchus was noted in v. 10, as was Barnabas's cousin Mark, in v. 10. One named "Jesus" who was called Justus was noted in v. 11. Epaphras then followed in v. 12, as did Luke and Demas in v. 14 and Nymphas in v. 15. Lastly, Paul mentioned Archippus in v. 17 and closed immediately thereafter. These were all men.

In the Colossian correspondence, Paul spoke principally about a man (Jesus) and to men—the Colossians. He commended right living to them and this entailed being kindly disposed toward their wives—a religious obligation in light of Jesus' service to and for humankind.

Paul and Women - Ephesians

Ephesians

Paul wrote to the Ephesians during his Roman imprisonment in 61/62AD. The famous epistle began with his standard salutation (1:1-2), after which he commenced to note privileges associated with membership in the commonwealth of Grace (1:3-3:21). The "battle of the sexes" wasn't developed in the Ephesians' text. Rather, here Paul placed a premium on battling forces within— the "flesh." In 4:1-6 he extolled the virtue of cooperation, a point further developed in vv. 7-16, culminating in an appeal for "the whole body being joined and knit together" (v. 16). Individuals were exhorted to keep distance between their former manner of lives, in vv. 17-32, a mandate followed by an exhortation to "walk in love," in 5:2. In 5:1-21, Paul pressed his constituents to walk in the light and not the darkness (see vv. 8-14), and then explicitly teased out applications for married life in subsequent verses.

In v. 22, wives were exhorted to "submit to" their "own husbands," and were reminded in v. 23 that "the husband is the head of the wife" (cf. v. 24). This then followed with an appeal for husbands to "love your wives" and to "give yourselves for her" in v. 24. After repeating the appeal, Paul closed saying: "husbands ought to love their own wives as their own bodies; for he who loves his wife loves himself." In v. 33 he offered the following summary: "let each of you in particular so love his wife as himself, and let the wife see that she respects her husband."

Woman By Divine Design

Paul's "headship" talk is understandingly problematic for many today. Can we Americans who have historically placed a premium on human autonomy since we stepped foot on these shores, and who have been appropriately suspicious of the excessive rights and rules of kings and rulers, really help but be any different? It seems not.

Against that backdrop, the master-and-slave language of dominance and submission, Lords and subjects, is problematic for us—not to mention its being anachronistic: perceived as a throwback to a bygone, bombastic era, it represents an unpleasant, medieval world, which no intelligent person would wish to return to.

While granting that the language invokes such images, we should not be too quick to judge it negatively. While granting that Paul advocated that husbands are to be the "head" of their wives, we do well to look more closely at the words he used—his words, not ours.

Two words are employed in the Greek language to denote heads: "*arche*" and "*kephale.*" Used as a prefix to denote "importance" and "power," "*arche*" is used in "archbishop," "archangel," and even "archenemy" to note the main person or persons—the head. Though the word is employed in the New Testament—to denote magistrates, chiefs, princes, rulers, and heads—it is not the word used by Paul in this case to spell out the nature of family leadership.[6]

Paul and Women - Ephesians

In this case, John Temple Bristow noted, in *What Paul Really Said About Women,* that "Paul did not choose the [authoritative] word *arche* when he wrote of how a husband is the head of his wife. He was well aware of that word, but he deliberately chose a different term. Instead, Paul used the word *kephale*. This word does mean head... [but i]t was never used to mean 'leader,' or 'boss,' or 'chief,' or 'ruler.' *Kephale* is also a military term, meaning one who 'leads,' but not in the sense of a [military] director... a 'general,' or a 'captain' who orders troops from a distance; quite the opposite, *kephale* was the one who went before the troops, the leader in the sense of being in the lead, [and thus] the first into battle."[7]

If Bristow's point prevails in our thinking—and there is a cogent argument that it should—one can surmise the following: Yes, the husband is the "head"; but "head" does not mean "dictator" as much as it denotes taking the lead and being the first into battle. That Paul advocated that husbands and wives serve each others' needs and interests underscores that Paul gave no place to pushy dictators, who believed that they possessed absolute authority on the basis of a misconstrued entitlement associated with the "Divine Rights of Husbands" as with "Kings." In like manner, that he requested "wives voluntarily, willingly, [and] actively be subject to their husbands" is something construed as being "voluntary by nature," and thus mitigates against the harsher reading.

Woman By Divine Design

In either case, "submit" is an awkward Greek term, one that could just as easily be rendered as "give allegiance to," "be responsive to," "tend to the needs of," and/or "place oneself at the disposition of."[8]

At first reading, Paul's anachronistic-sounding language seems overly domineering—and thus out of keeping with sentiments in the modern era. However, a more deliberate rendering of his thoughts shows him to be a liberator of womankind, and forcefully reflects the intentions of a fellow given to advocating for a balance of power in marriage and not the subjugation of one spouse over the other.

This is the *real* Paul! The other is a fantasy foisted upon us by those who would see the Scriptures discredited.

Paul and Women - Philippians

Philippians

As with Philemon, Colossians, and Ephesians, Paul is said to have written his Philippian correspondence during his Roman imprisonment in 62AD. This was a "thank you" letter, written to express gratitude for their unyielding financial support (4:10-20). The Philippians were the most loyal of Paul's followers, keeping steady till the end of his life and ministry. Paul established the church there during his second missionary journey, with a "core group" of female followers. In Acts 16: 12-15, Luke said: we "were staying in that city for some days. And on the Sabbath day we went out of the city [of Philippi] to the riverside, where prayer was customarily made; and we sat down and *spoke to the women who met there.*" After noting that women gathered for a synagogue service and that Paul was kindly disposed toward them (evident from his sitting among them and conversing with them), Luke informed in v. 14 that "a certain woman named Lydia heard us…," and that, "the Lord opened her heart to heed the things spoken by Paul." That she was a woman of means and influence is attested in v. 15, where Luke noted that "her household" was subsequently baptized, and that she unilaterally urged Paul to "come to my house" to stay.

The Philippian correspondence was Paul's most gentle. Therein, we do not hear him offering a word against anyone or anything, for he is only saying "thanks." That the recipient group was apparently initially constituted by females is interesting, as is the fact that Paul seemed to enjoy the company of well-placed and powerful women. That he enjoyed the respect of influential women, as per Acts 17:4 where "leading women joined Paul," underscores that he left a reasonably powerful impression on his female hearers, partly because his was a liberating message, one that placed more of a premium on equality than was typically offered in the marketplace of religious ideas. In return, women supported Paul financially, prayerfully, and socially. In many ways a disrespected man, Paul most likely appreciated the support he received from women, and we can only expect that he would repay their kindness with kindness.

Paul and Women – 1 Timothy

1 Timothy

Paul penned his first letter to Timothy after the Roman imprisonment, which served as the backdrop for some of the aforementioned correspondences. He warned against heresies in 1:3-20, after which he gave instructions for facilitating a growing Church in 2:1-3:13. Paul's recipe for success included, but was not limited to, attending to public prayer (2:1-8), women maintaining proper comportment (2:9-15), and leaders marshalling the resources necessary to develop good character (3:1-13). Having discussed issues associated with the Christian family and the Christian leader, Paul goes on to exhort Timothy to keep to the orthodox faith (3:14-4:16) and to faithfully pastor the church's constituents in 5:1-6:2b. Having dealt some with home and church, Paul starts his wrap-up with a consideration of employee-employer relations (6:1-2), closing with an addendum that the Church is to accept no other practices, and that those who advocate otherwise know nothing (vv. 3-16). He closes saying: "O Timothy! Guard what was committed to your trust, avoiding profane and idle babblings and contradictions of what is commonly called knowledge—by professing it some have strayed concerning the faith…" (vv. 20-21).

Paul's most troubling women's passage is found in 2:8-15. The somewhat lengthy quote is reproduced below in its New King James Version form. After getting the full passage in view, a negatively inclined rendering of it will be presented, which argues for the silencing and subjugation of womankind. After giving voice to that perspective—not one held by the authors—other interpretive options will be considered, affording readers the opportunity to possibly see the old wording in a new light.

Paul said:

> 8 I desire… 9 that the women adorn themselves in modest apparel, with propriety and moderation, not with braided hair or gold or pearls or costly clothing, 10 but, which is proper for women professing godliness, with good works. 11 Let a woman learn in silence, with all submission. 12 And I do not permit a woman to teach or have authority over a man, but to be in silence. 13 For Adam was formed first, then Eve. 14 And Adam was not deceived, but the woman being deceived fell into transgression. 15 Nevertheless, she will be saved in childbearing if they continue in faith, love, and holiness, with self-control.

Verses 8-10 do not stand out as being particularly problematic. The encouragement to wear modest apparel and not be too glitzy was an oft-repeated exhortation in antiquity—as it should be now. Who hasn't been to a shopping mall and taken note of what the young girls are wearing today? Might the girls be better served were someone to tell them to put some real clothes on? So it would seem. Paul was keen on the need for propriety. That coupled with the fact that Paul underscored the necessity for males, in like manner, to hold themselves "in check" reasonably well, in 3:1-13, doesn't make Paul

Paul and Women – 1 Timothy

sound like a women-hater. What follows does, however, and to that we will attend.

In 2:11, Paul said that a woman should "learn in silence" and be in "submission" to her husband. In v. 12 he frankly said, "I do not permit a woman to have authority over a man," after which he again underscored that she should "be in silence." The theological basis for his teaching isn't rooted in his own authority—which one could suppose he might have claimed as an Apostle; to the contrary, he harked back to a primeval story, handed down by Moses.

Why should a woman be silent and not get the better of the men? In v. 13, Paul wrote that "Adam was formed first, then Eve." From there, in v. 14, he opined that "Adam was not deceived" but the woman was; she, in turn, led Adam into temptation, which resulted in "the fall of man"—and woman. Having offered the above as proof that women are not capable of leading men and must be dutifully submissive to them—presumably, lest they repeat the offenses of their mother, Eve—Paul then graciously says, "she will be saved in childbearing, if they continue in faith, love, and holiness, with self-control." As if what preceded wasn't insulting enough, Paul digs a deeper hole for himself saying, in effect: "Oh, you women should just have children and concentrate on raising them; if you hold them to faith, love, and holiness, you can save your sinfully-inclined souls."

Is this what Paul really said about women? If so, it is no surprise that many female readers walk away from the

Woman By Divine Design

Text feeling slighted by Christianity. Paul, Christianity's primary spokesman, seems to belittle women, urging their "silence," underscoring the unacceptability of their having "authority over men," and their need to be "in submission" to men (vv. 11-12). In support of this position, in vv. 13-14 Paul harks back to Adam and Eve and seems to blame Eve for sin's making its entrance onto the stage of the human drama. The upshot, according to this interpretation, is that women have no recourse but to dutifully rear children, being incapable of doing much else.

Having listened to the disparaging assessment of Paul on women, let's begin with the end of Paul's argument and see if the aforementioned perspective can hold up in the light of scrutiny.

How does one square Paul's seeming to blame the woman for Adam's and the world's ills (v. 14) with Paul's statements in Romans 5 that, "*through one man* sin entered the world" (v. 12), that this sin "reigned *from Adam*" (v. 14) and that "*through one man's offense death reigned*" in v. 17a. Here, he lays the blame for the race's defilement at Adam's feet, not Eve's, does he not?

If Paul does *not* believe that women are to be blamed for the race's miseries, then arguing for female subjugation and silence on the basis of that assumption could *not* have been his intention. So, what was?

Paul and Women – 1 Timothy

In the Genesis narrative, Adam is created first. In 2:15, God "took the man and put him in the Garden of Eden," and then instructed him in vv. 16-17: "The Lord God commanded the man, saying, 'Of every tree of the Garden you may freely eat; but of the tree of the knowledge of good and evil you shall not eat, for in the day that you eat of it you shall die." The point is that God gave these instructions to Adam—*before* there ever was an Eve. His wife had no firsthand knowledge of the commandment.

Following on the heels of the Divine mandate in Genesis came the following: "And the Lord God said, 'It is not good for a man to be alone; I will make him a helper comparable to him'" (v. 18). What was this!? Adam never saw anything like this before! She presented herself to him in v. 22b, in response to which he happily exclaimed: "This is now bone of my bones and flesh of my flesh" (v. 23), or, in the vernacular, "Now, that's what I'm talking about!" Excited and distracted as he was by her presence, he was more inclined to please her than to attend to his business, and this proved disastrous. That men can become easily distracted by women is amply attested in both Sacred Scripture and in secular experience, is it not?

Eve didn't directly hear the instructions about the tree and its forbidden fruit; all she heard was Adam's recollection and instructions—which she disregarded. Adam heard God's instructions and was particularly responsible.

Woman By Divine Design

With no firsthand knowledge, Eve could be more easily manipulated—and she was.

We're told that "the serpent was more cunning than any beast of the field... And *he said to the woman*, 'Has God indeed said 'You shall not eat of every tree of the garden'?" (3:1) First, it was intended to be a confusing question. God never said that one can't eat from "every tree," but that one must not eat from a particular tree. She was knocked off balance intentionally. After attempting to straighten him out in vv. 2-3, the "deceiver" came out more forcefully and said, in effect, "You've got it all wrong, Mrs. Adam. No harm will befall you... In fact you'll be all the better for eating of this fruit, as will your husband!" (See vv. 4-5) She ate in v. 6, after which "she also gave to her husband with her, and he ate."

While granting that Paul references the story—primarily to underscore the Jewish perspective that a man is principally responsible to get his arms around biblical instruction and, in turn, is responsible to take it home and give it to the family—*he is not disparaging womankind* by telling it. In the Jewish tradition, boys were much more educated in the ways of the Torah and were, thus, held to a higher standard.

As for the "silencing" of women, one wonders how Paul could say "I do not permit a woman to teach or have authority over a man" (v. 12), given his ubiquitous acknowledgment of women's assisting in the growth and development of the Church in other parts of his writings.

Paul and Women – 1 Timothy

As has been noted, over and again, Paul and his traveling assistant, Luke, commended women, noted that some served in leadership roles, as prophetesses and deaconesses, and even credited some with helping to instruct male leaders. Luke, you'll remember, wrote that Priscilla helped tutor Apollos; and later, addressing Timothy in his follow-up epistle, Paul commended Timothy's mother and grandmother, saying that his confidence in Timothy was, in part, attributed to knowing that these women had instructed him.

Given the newly found freedom that women had "in Christ," it may well be that some women went overboard in the fellowship—prompting Paul to "tone it down" some. Regardless, Paul's saying that "women should not teach or have authority over men" could be better rendered as "women should not disciple men." At issue is *mentoring toward manhood* and preparing for leadership: for these tasks, men are better helped along by men. In like manner, Paul would say that the "older women should instruct the younger ones" on matters of love, the home, dealing with husbands, etc. While men can and should be influenced by women, it is better that men be mentored to maturity by other men, and women by women. Is this sexism, or is it common sense?

His calling for some women to "be silent" could have been a rebuke to some who were "out of bounds," or it could mean that women should "be at rest," or "be still," or some such less disparaging term. While there was room for women's voices and views both in Paul's personal world and in the congregations under his sway, Paul would obviously prefer that men step forth, lead, and guide the churches into the future.

Is Paul's saying that women will "be saved through childbearing" relegating females to a subservient role, or is he simply saying that women are designed for motherhood and for employing leadership prerogatives in the home and on their families' behalf, over endeavoring to be the principal leaders of the fledgling churches? That men and women are constituted differently is well attested in nature, and Paul should not be discriminated against for having brought the obvious to our attention.

The Greek word for "saved," for that matter, should not be construed as "soul-saved"—as in "Are you saved, 'born again'?"—but rather should be more broadly construed as referring to one's being "healed," "made whole," and "completed." At issue is women's finding more fulfillment and wholeness in attending to the homefront, against being overly invested in the Church's corporate business—what the men are wired for. That the better part of the letter considers various roles and functions underscores that Paul is not making a particular point about women—for he speaks much more about men—as much as he is simply trying to provide a framework for good order in the home and in the church.

Paul and Women – Titus

Titus

Paul wrote Titus in 63/64 AD, shortly after his Roman imprisonment. As was the case in 1 Timothy, in the Titus correspondence he addressed leadership qualifications, in 1:5-9, and then swiftly picked up on problems with bad leaders, false teachers who lead others astray (1:10-16). In 2:1ff. he commended good doctrine (v. 1), exhorted the old (vv. 2-3) and the young (vv. 4-8), and then extolled the virtue of a good work ethic (vv. 9-10). Women's issues do surface briefly in this short piece. In 2:3-5, Paul bid that older women be "reverent in behavior, not slanderers, nor given to much wine, teachers of good things—that they admonish the young women to love their husbands, to love their children, to be discreet, chaste, homemakers, obedient to their husbands." Paul exhorted the Believers toward good works, in 11-15, and advocated for compliance with government in 3:1, as with the necessity of governing one's own affairs properly (vv. 2-11). Paul's adumbration of his previously noted concerns came naturally to him in the context of the overall letter. He wasn't given to singling out women, as much as he was simply going through his predictable lists—e.g., looking at men and women, the old and young, masters and slaves, and the like…. Lists are good. He was specific, letting individuals know exactly what was expected.

As for the women's issues specifically, his command to be "reverent in behavior" and to "not [be] slanderers" was also given to men, who were forever urged by him throughout chapter 3 to respect each other, as with authorities both inside and outside of the Church. Much as he exhorted the women not to be given to wine, he did so with men, whom he also exhorted to be "teachers of good things." His "admonish[ing] the young women to love their husbands, to love their children, to be discreet, chaste, homemakers, obedient to their husbands" parrots his instructions to husbands in Eph. 5 to "love their wives as Christ loved the Church." Here as elsewhere, Paul seems principally concerned with the maintenance of good order in various social systems: family networks, employment networks, government networks, and the like.

Paul and Women – 2 Timothy

2 Timothy

Paul wrote his final letter in 66/67AD, just prior to his death—which he, at that juncture, was anticipating. In 4:6-8 he gives voice to his being ready to be an "offering," stating that the "time of my departure is at hand" (v. 6). Timothy was likely disconcerted, a state of mind that probably prompted Paul to write.

In 1:3-2:7 he reflected on his longstanding, personal relationship with Timothy. Paul reminded him that the "genuine faith" that was in Timothy, "dwelt first in your grandmother Lois and your mother Eunice." Paul wanted him to "stir up the gift of God" resident within him (v. 6), with a follow-up that "God has not given us a spirit of fear, but of power and of love and of a sound mind" (v. 7). After firing Timothy's courage, in part, by beckoning to his mother's and grandmother's examples, Paul exhorted him now to "not be ashamed of the testimony" (v. 8) and then to "hold fast the pattern of sound words" given to him (v. 13). Paul went on to encourage steadfastness by employing illustrations from warfare (2:3-4), athletics (v. 5), and farming (v. 6). He then addressed false teachers (2:14-26) and reminded that perilous times are coming (3:1-9). Against this backdrop, Paul exhorted Timothy, saying: "continue in the things you have learned" (3:14), while noting that "from childhood you have known the Holy Scriptures" (v. 15). And how was it that Timothy became acquainted with those Scriptures? It was a testimony to his grandmother's and mother's influences, to be sure. Paul wrapped up the letter exhorting him to "preach the Word!" as he had been taught it (4:2), despite the fact that people will disappoint and abandon (vv. 3-5). The Lord is faithful, however: In v. 17, Paul testified that "the Lord stood with me and strengthened me, so that the message might be preached fully through me." He then commended Christ to Timothy's spirit and closed (v. 22).

Paul and Women – Summary

Summary: Paul and Women
How do Paul's writings contribute toward our understanding of women by Divine design?

On one level, it could be said that Paul doesn't make much of a contribution, given the fact that he doesn't typically "weigh in" on women's issues in his writings. When he does, it is usually when he is troubleshooting problems associated with individual fledgling congregations: he was constantly being called upon to put out brushfires and to mediate squabbles. His even occasional mention of women typically appears in the context of his running down an essential qualities list for men, for women, for the old and the young, for servants and masters, etc. Though he doesn't, on the whole, go out of his way to focus on women, he does focus on them occasionally. In his writings, he takes issue with domineering prophetesses, who—as with the pagan sorts—tended to want to run the prophetic show. His letters were passed around the early churches and continue to be useful because, though they addressed specific conditions of a specific congregation, those conditions didn't remain unique, but became widespread concerns.

Paul makes room for spiritual gifts and for women being in the possession of those gifts. He is heard allowing for women to employ their gifts in corporate gatherings, but he does so with the provision that the *women work alongside their husbands and the Church leadership,* which he is forever trying to strengthen. While speaking of "strengthening," it seems that the few times Paul does take up gender issues, he does so with the purpose of facilitating marriages for the singles and for strengthening existing unions of those already paired.

What Paul said about women, he said to clarify their role in God's design for order in the family and the Church. *How* Paul said it was aimed at the particular brushfire he was fighting and the audience of his day. How his words have been *interpreted* in different Bible translations and denominations depended on the historical and political prism of the translator. That's why we examined the original Greek of Paul's letters to ascertain his *intent*.

What we need to recognize is that women were respected in Paul's inner world, and that he exhorted other men to respect and cherish women, as well. Paul benefited from associations with many women, whom he construed as able co-workers; he was given to freely crediting them in his writings—as was his protégé, Luke.

Conclusion

Jesus' words are clear and timeless and studying their context is insightful. Paul framed his words for each particular audience's situation and study of their context is essential to render his meaning timeless. Having focused upon what Jesus and Paul said to, for, and about women, and having briefly considered some of the context within which they spoke, let us conclude now by revisiting the Texts wherein they spoke *directly* about God's Divine design for women.

In chapter 10, Mark traced Jesus' footsteps as He made His way to Jerusalem, recalling Jesus' dealing with divorce along the way, in vv. 1-12.

In response to the question "Is it lawful for a man to divorce his wife?" Jesus appealed to Moses in v. 3, asking, "What did Moses command you?" Men correctly answered that "Moses permitted a man to write a certificate of divorce and to dismiss her" (v. 4), in response to which Jesus said it was still *not* God's Divine design from the beginning (vv. 6-9). The implication, of course, is that He does not favor the practice.

Mark's story was replicated by Matthew in 19:1-10 where, in the wake of Jesus' saying that marriage should be binding, and giving no place whatsoever to casual

Woman By Divine Design

divorces (vv. 4-9), the male disciples asked why they should bother to marry, in v. 10. Jesus informed that castrated men needn't worry about marriage; those who are not castrated, however, need to come to terms with the fact that they are duty bound to stay with their wives.

Those interested in following Jesus' teachings should note that a man is not entitled to the pleasures of sexual experience if he is not minded to attend to the treasures that come as a result—the inviolate union with his spouse and the responsibilities associated with the children that inevitably come as a result of their union.

Jesus' explicit appeal to Divine design here was in the context of eschewing divorcement. Noteworthy is the fact that Divine design for womankind is framed in the context of *connection* with men. The men, in like manner, are instructed that, while there are exceptions to every rule, it is *generally preferable* for a man to be in union with a woman, and not alone. Jesus is on record commending an inviolate interrelationship between men and women as the "Gold Standard." Is there a Divine design for womankind apart from this construct? Again, there are exceptions to every rule, but those who take note of nature and Scripture are still forced to conclude that the *design is found in connection and not in distinction.*

Paul appealed directly to Divine design in 1 Tim. 2:8-15. In the first three verses he said, "8 I desire... 9 that the women adorn themselves in modest apparel, with propriety

Conclusion

and moderation, not with braided hair or gold or pearls or costly clothing, 10 but, which is proper for women professing godliness, with good works."

Women are shown here to exact considerable influence over the males of the species, testosterone-driven as they are. Against this backdrop, women are exhorted not to use appearance to gain undo leverage over men to facilitate connection, but to represent themselves discreetly and to carry themselves with the dignity that befits religious virtue.

Savvy women know all too well the leveraging ability inherent in their natural appearance. Paul counsels that women not display and accentuate their natural attributes to facilitate unions that are not in keeping with God's ultimate purpose for them. Single men can figure out what a woman looks like without all the showy embellishments. Paul advocates that it is better for women of faith to keep themselves in reserve and, thus, garner the attention of a prospective mate based on assorted inner characteristics and not just outer ones. This is not sexist talk; it is sage father-daughter advice. In Paul's correspondences, over and again, men are exhorted to behave in like manner, and thus to keep relationships with the opposite sex unsullied.

Let's take a fresh look at the next verses, 11 and 12. Using the language of our new understanding Paul said, "A woman should get her religious instruction from the men of the Church and from older women, who also learned from and teach others under the guidance of the Church leaders and older women. Women should not

Woman By Divine Design

guide a young man into manhood; that is the duty of the men around him. Women should guide younger women into womanhood." The reason for this was spelled out, beginning in v. 13. Again in our new language: "Lest one think that it is just testosterone-driven men who are prone to sway, a weakened woman—Eve—let unbridled greed sway her judgment. She drifted off course and went after the forbidden fruit. This naked woman then used her influence to entice Adam, who subsequently succumbed to the temptation as well."

Sin entered by means of the aforementioned transaction, and the race was corrupted—by *both* man and woman. Having been saved from the ravages of sin through the Messiah, women and men are now invited to find their place *together* in a paradise restored.

Paul employed the Adam and Eve story both to underscore the responsibility Jewish men traditionally assumed with their advanced religious education, and to lead into v. 15 in which he counseled (using our new language), that *women will find their fulfillment through their unique design to bear and influence children and by working alongside their men and religious leaders*, as opposed to operating apart from them—as was the case with some prophetess-types in Paul's day.

Legitimized marriage was construed by Paul as the principal context within which women and men find human fulfillment, together. Though his words are often misunderstood by many, Paul made room in his world—

Conclusion

more than most others did—for women to be involved in good work outside the home; this is evident throughout Paul's writings.

As did Jesus, Paul used language of his own to advocate for *connectivity* in Divine design. Men and women both carry charges—an electrical magnetism—that incline them to connect with each other. The necessity of figuring out how to work together in the wake of being bound together is the point driven repeatedly. Paul bids the older women to help the younger to come to terms with this, much as the older men are exhorted to help the younger men.

Irrespective of a woman's social status—single, married, divorced, or widowed—women are esteemed in the biblical narrative. Women are every bit as much Children of God as are men, and because of this have certain privileges.

This is God's design for an ideal world. The world isn't "ideal," but that doesn't mean we shouldn't know God's plan and aspire to it. Jesus and Paul acted on their own advice and modeled the actions and attitudes that make it easier for us to live together.

Bible readers are led to the conclusion that all women are invited to work at advancing the Messiah's Kingdom, to the end that His Kingdom come and His will be done on Earth as it is in Heaven.

Endnotes

page 2: [1] R. Laird Harris, Gleason Archer, Bruce K. Waltke, *Theological Wordbook of the Old Testament* (Chicago: Moody Press, 1980), pp. 595-596.

page 2: [2] Culled from James Strong, A Concise Dictionary of Words in the Greek New Testament (MacDonald Publishing Company), p. 36; and W. E. Vine, A Comprehensive Dictionary of the Original Greek Words with their Precise Meanings for English Readers (MacDonald Publishing Company), pp. 430, 1250-1251.

page 56: [3] Muller, H., *Freedom in the Ancient World* (New York: Harper and Row, 1961), pp. 318-319; culled from Bristow, John T., *What Paul Really Said About Women* (San Francisco: Harper and Row, 1988), p. 1.

page 61: [4] As with both the Galatian text (above) and 2 Thessalonians (which follows), Paul mentions nobody by name. This will change. In his later writings, he commends a variety by name—some of them women.

page 75: [5] Much as there are discernible differences between the other categories.

page 78: [6] Bristow John T., *What Paul Really Said About Women* (San Francisco: Harper and Row, 1988), pp. 35-36.

page 79: [7] Ibid., pp. 36-37

page 80: [8] Ibid., p. 40.

Glossary of Women Noted in the Text

Anna: prophetess daughter of Phanuel, from the tribe of Asher. After only seven years of marriage, Anna became a widow and thereafter devoted herself to serving the Lord in His Temple, day and night. At age 84, Anna met the infant Messiah and thereafter proclaimed her Redeemer. **39-40**

Apphia: Philemon's wife and hostess for the church that met at their house. Tradition says she was stoned to death under Nero's persecution of Christians. 73-74

Bathsheba: a very beautiful woman, daughter of Eliam, wife of Uriah the Hittite; then, wife of King David, mother of King Solomon. 23, **27-28**

Chloe: a wealthy woman in Corinth who sent some of her household to consult Paul. 63

Crippled "Daughter of Abraham:" her Sabbath healing by Jesus exposed to all the people the emptiness of the religious leaders' claims to represent God. 43-44

Elizabeth: a descendant of Aaron and the wife of Zechariah, the priest who was visited by the angel Gabriel. A reverent woman, joyously devoted to her Lord, an older relative of the Virgin Mary, and barren until God showed His favor and she gave birth to John the Baptist. When visited by Mary, Elizabeth told her that Mary was the mother of the Lord. 37-38, 40

Woman By Divine Design

Eunice: Timothy's mother, Jewish wife of a Greek husband. It is likely that she and Lois (see below) came to faith on Paul's first visit to Lystra, because Timothy seemed already familiar with Paul's persecution there. 89, 93

Eve: the first woman was created in God's image, thus sharing with Adam the source of all human dignity which differentiates humans from the rest of the animal kingdom. God's intention in her creation—taken out of man—was that she complement Adam, implying an incompleteness to man without woman. The absence of woman from creation, in fact, brought a declaration from God of "not good" (Gen 2:18). Women were designed by God to share in a mutuality with men based on their simultaneous similarity and dissimilarity. 1, 85-88, 100

Herodias: niece of Herod Philip and Herod Antipas, she divorced one to marry the other and invoked the condemnation of John the Baptist. She successfully conspired for John's death, using her daughter, Salomé (below). She and Antipas were eventually banished to Gaul. 31

Jairus' daughter: ailing twelve-year-old girl whose powerful father pleaded with Jesus to save her. She died before Jesus arrived, but His touch healed her. 17, 30

Joanna, wife of Chuza (Herod's steward): had been healed by Jesus and, with other women similarly healed, helped to provide for Jesus and His ministry out of their own means. 42-43

Glossary of Women Noted in the Text

Julia: a Christian woman who lived in Rome and was greeted by Paul. 71

Junia: with her husband, Andronicus, a "fellow prisoner" with Paul and acknowledged by Paul to be "in Christ before me." 70, 71

Lois: Timothy's grandmother, (see Eunice above). Although little is known of Lois and Eunice, their influence on Timothy, instilling in him the love of the Lord, was praised by Paul. 89, 93

Martha: sister of Lazarus and Mary, and with them, a dear friend and faithful disciple of Jesus. They lived in Bethany and Jesus frequently visited them when He was in Jerusalem, staying with them during His last week on Earth. Distracted by her daily tasks, Martha was so busy preparing for Jesus' visit that she missed out on the close fellowship with Him that her brother and sister enjoyed. Her honesty and steadfast faith were revealed when Jesus arrived after Lazarus had died. Martha told Jesus how she felt, but exercised faith in His ability to help. Jesus honored her faith and raised Lazarus from the dead. 49, **50**

Mary, mother of Jesus: Little is said of her in the Sacred Text. From the biblical sources, however, we know that her life was characterized by faith, humility, and obedience to the will of God. A descendant of King David—many scholars contend that the genealogy in Luke is Mary's and the one in Matthew is Joseph's. 23, **28-30**, 35, **37-40**, 47-48, 50-51

Woman By Divine Design

Mary Magdalene: a woman from Magdala, a town near Tiberias. Jesus removed evil spirits from her and she joined His ministry, supporting it from her own resources. Following her vigil at the foot of the cross, she was the first to see Him after His resurrection. Because of her constancy throughout Jesus' ministry (in the Scriptures she is mentioned by name 14 times), some refer to her as "apostle to the Apostles." In 591 AD, Mary Magdalene was officially construed as the prostitute delivered by Jesus, by Pope Gregory I when he combined her character with the sinful woman mentioned just before her in Luke 7, as anointing the Lord's feet with oil from an alabaster jar. This label lasted 1,400 years until the Roman Catholic Church recanted it and canonized Saint Mary Magdalene in 1969. Textual evidence is Spartan and we know little about her. 21, 35, 42, 50.

Mary: sister of Lazarus and Martha, and with them, close friend of Jesus and faithful disciple. She was involved in three events: (1) when she sat at Jesus' feet listening to Him while Martha worked in the kitchen, (2) when she fell at Jesus' feet to plead for her brother's life, and (3) when, during His last week, she anointed Jesus' feet with costly oil and wiped them with her hair. In each event, Jesus affirmed that His teaching and His work was for people like her. 49, 50

Mary, mother of James and Joses, wife of Clopas, sister of Jesus' mother, eyewitness to the crucifixion and present at His tomb on Resurrection morning. With other women,

Glossary of Women Noted in the Text

she carried the news of the Resurrection to the disciples, also called "the other Mary." 21, 50

Mary (Mariam): a Jewess greeted by Paul in his letter to the Romans. 70, 71

Naomi: best known as Ruth's (see below) mother-in-law, Naomi had hope and God provided. **25-26**

Nereus' sister: a Christian greeted by Paul in his letter to the Romans. 71

Orpah: one of Naomi's two daughters-in-law (see Ruth below). 25-26

Persis: greeted as a Christian woman who "worked very hard in the Lord," by Paul in his letter to the Romans. 71

Peter's mother-in-law: She had a serious, high fever and Jesus touched her hand. Jews believed that touching a sick person would make them unclean. By means of touching, Jesus demonstrated that He can touch sick people without becoming unclean because His touch heals them. We get a glimpse of her character when, after her healing, she served Jesus and some of His Disciples. In the Gospels, serving is a sign of greatness. **17**, 30

Phoebe: called "deaconess" by Paul, it is clear that he had a high regard for her work for the Lord. Paul's urging that she be helped in any way possible indicated that she had a specific role to perform. An order of deaconesses existed in the 2nd century. This is the principal New Testament reference to such a position. **70**

Priscilla: married to a Jewish tentmaker, Aquila; they are always mentioned together. Because of the Edict of Claudius, they left Rome for Corinth in 49AD where Aquila and Paul worked as tentmakers and Paul lived in their home. They accompanied Paul to Syria and settled in Ephesus where they met Apollos, a Jew preaching Jesus in the synagogue who was very knowledgeable about Scriptures, but who knew only of the baptism of John. Priscilla and Aquila invited him into their home and taught him how John's message pointed to Jesus. Priscilla was an intelligent woman, and in no way was perceived as being inferior to her husband in knowledge or service. With him, she was a vital part of the Church's ministry in the 1st century. She was faithful, supportive to her husband, hospitable, and honorable, and was honored by Paul, time and time again, for these and other reasons. **66, 70-71, 89**

Rahab: the God-fearing prostitute used by God to further His plan, mother of Boaz, progenitor of Jesus. Rahab's commitment to Joshua's invading Israelites and their Lord was a commitment of faith included in the Old Testament and acknowledged in the New Testament. **23-25**

Rachel: wife of Jacob, mother of Joseph and Benjamin (during whose birth she died). She and Jacob were one of the great love matches in the Bible. Though jealous of

Glossary of Women Noted in the Text

her sister Leah's easy fertility, she had a tender heart. It was Rachel whom Jeremiah heard weeping for her exiled children. 2

Rebekah: mother of twins, Esau and Jacob, she enjoyed a happy marriage with Isaac. She proved to be an industrious woman, one given to looking out for her interests. Preferring Jacob over Esau, she schemed to direct the Lord's "first born" promise to and through Jacob, and obtained Isaac's blessing for Jacob. The Lord worked through her endeavors, given Esau's proving to be unfit for the tribe's headship. She and Isaac are buried at Machpelah in Hebron. 1-2

Rufus's mother: greeted by Paul in Romans, she had apparently looked after Paul on occasion as Paul refers to her as "Rufus' mother and mine." 71

Ruth: a Moabite gentile, she followed Naomi and adopted her God, winning the heart of Boaz and eventually and providentially entered into the direct line of Jesus. It is remarkable that Ruth plays such an important role in the biblical record. Moab and Israel had such hostile relations that the Lord even forbade any Moabite from entering the assembly of the Lord. Ruth's presence can only be due to God's providence, evidence of His Grace and ability to work in and through the life of anyone, no matter their background. Ruth's goodness and righteousness were rewarded with a new husband, a son, and the blessing of standing in the lineage of Jesus Christ. That the beautiful narrative has the name of Ruth is unusual as

Woman By Divine Design

Esther and Ruth are the only books named after women, and Ruth is the sole book bearing the name of a gentile in all of Scripture. 23, **25-26**

Salomé: one of the women who watched the crucifixion at a distance and who, after the burial, anointed Jesus' body with spices. 21

Salomé: daughter of Herodias (according to Josephus, the historian), who danced for Herod Antipas and was rewarded with her wish: the head of John the Baptist. **31**

Samaritan woman at the well: her encounter with Jesus demonstrated two truths—(1) Jesus' divine ability to search the human heart and reveal God's truth, and (2) that those who worship God, regardless of ethnicity, must do so in spirit and in truth. 48-49

Sarah: an paradigm of wifely respect as she followed her husband, Abraham, when he answered God's call into an unknown land. Her inability to bear a child prompted her to offer her handmaiden to Abraham, the consequences of which are felt today. 1

Sinner with alabaster jar: entered, uninvited, the home of a Pharisee and anointed Jesus' feet early in His ministry. 41-42

Susanna: one of the women who supported Jesus out of her own means during His earthly ministry. 42

Glossary of Women Noted in the Text

Syro-Phoenician: Mark went to great lengths to inform us that she was a pagan: she was both Greek and, by race, a Phoenician. In a testy manner, and in response to her request for help, Jesus declared his mission to the children of Israel, not to the unclean gentile "dogs." The woman's determination seemed to place her in direct conflict with Jesus' expressed priority to fulfill God's mission with Israel. While this exchange may well have foreshadowed the confrontation between the disciples and the pagan world, it also illustrated the undeserved and often unexpected nature of God's Grace to all people. The encounter expands the hope that participation in God's Kingdom is possible for the gentiles after all. 20, 32

Tamar: daughter-in-law of Judah, mother of his twin boys, Perez and Zerah, by subterfuge. **23-24**

Tryphena and Tryphosa: two women greeted by Paul in Romans, who had sacrificed to work for the Lord. 71

Widow of Nain: early in the second year of Jesus' public ministry and right after the Sermon on the Mount, Jesus performed his first raising of the dead on the only son of this widow, demonstrating His compassion and illustrating for John the Baptist's disciples that "the dead are raised." 40

Woman with blood-related problem: her unfortunate illness rendered her as "unclean" and cast her as an outcast in Israel. Contrary to custom, driven by faith in who Jesus was and what He could do, she touched Him,

Woman By Divine Design

and did so in an open space. By way of reponse, Jesus made an example of her, treating her not only as having worth, but as doing a faithful thing. He relieved her of any sense of guilt for her seemingly rash act and sent her on her way as a powerful witness to God's power and grace in the new economy. **17-19**, 30

Woman-focused Parables:
Ten Virgins: reminder that Believers must keep vigilant and be prepared to meet the Lord at any moment. 34

Widow and the unjust judge: Through sheer persistence she wears down an unscrupulous judge until he gives her justice. With this parable, Jesus illustrates how God as our Judge is much quicker to bestow His justice, blessing, and help when we need it, and will respond if we pray with expectant faith and confidence in God's merciful care and providence. 45-46

Woman of the Lost Coin: with this story and the parable of the Lost Sheep, Jesus insisted that sinners must be sought out and not merely mourned. God does not rejoice in the loss of anyone, but desires that all be saved and restored to fellowship with Him. That is why the whole community of Heaven rejoices when one sinner is found and restored to fellowship with God. 44

Study Guide

After reading the chapter on **Jesus and Women**, answer the following questions:

1. What biblical passages most illuminate the relationship between Jesus and women?

2. If you are a woman, which women do you identify with in the stories and why?

3. Which attributes are most significant?

4. How might you model some of those attributes and contribute toward God's work?

Study Guide

5. List other women of the Bible who seem to reflect those attributes as well.

6. Do any contemporary women come to mind who reflect the kinds of virtues noted and deemed admirable?

Woman By Divine Design

7. How might you imitate them?

Study Guide

After reading the chapter on **Paul and Women**, answer the following questions:

1. What biblical passages most illuminate the relationship between Paul and women?

2. According to Paul, how are women and men "One in the Messiah"?

3. According to Paul, how are men and women different?

4. How is Paul misinterpreted today?

Study Guide

5. How did Paul advocate for women's freedoms?

6. According to Paul, what is God's Divine design for womankind?